The Lucky Ones
Legacy of Norbert Gerling, World War II Tank Destroyer

Jeremy Paul Ämick

Yorkshire Publishing

The Lucky Ones
Copyright © 2019 by Jeremy Paul Ämick.

ISBN: 978-1-950034-11-6

All rights reserved.

No part of this publication may be reproduced, distributed, or transmitted in any form or by any means, including photocopying, recording, or other electronic or mechanical methods, without the prior written permission of the publisher, except in the case of brief quotations embodied in critical reviews and certain other noncommercial uses permitted by copyright law.

For permission requests, write to the publisher at the address below.

Yorkshire Publishing
4613 E. 91st St.
Tulsa, Oklahoma 74137
www.YorkshirePublishing.com
918.394.2665

Table of Contents

Acknowledgements ... *v*
Dedication ... *vii*
Introduction ... *ix*

CHAPTER ... PAGE

1 Humble beginnings ... 1
2 From the farm to the "Hellcat" ... 11
3 The War in Europe ... 29
4 Recreation ... 41
5 Battle of the Bulge ... 47
6 Germany and beyond ... 65
7 Ready for home ... 83
8 A return to the quiet life ... 93

Works Cited ... *117*
Index ... *125*

Acknowledgements

As is generally the case with any historical and literary endeavor, there are scores of individuals and organizations that helped contribute through their knowledge, support or resources. First, I must thank Norbert Gerling for his time and patience during the many interviews he endured over a two-year period. Secondly, I would like to extend my appreciation to the scores of volunteers who have helped research the graves and burials that are listed on the *Find A Grave* website; your dedication to preserving this facet of our nation's history greatly assisted me in locating information regarding many of the soldiers with whom Norbert Gerling served. Furthermore, I am always appreciative of the efforts of the Missouri Secretary of State's office for their detailed and focused work in preserving and sharing the military history of our state by making the birth and death certificates, and military service records, of thousands of Missourians available online and through their archives.

Dedication

To the memory of my dear friend, Norbert Gerling. Thank you for the many hours you spent sharing your story of service. You were certainly one of the "Greatest Generation" and deeply missed by many. Until we meet again ...

Introduction

When I first met Norbert Gerling in his rural Cole County, Missouri home in 2014, I was amazed at the dexterity, energy and detailed memories possessed by the *then* ninety-five-year-old combat veteran. As he proudly exclaimed, "I still cut my own firewood and spend my days working around the farm," it did not require a doctorate in an obscure medical discipline to realize that this was a man who, after more than nine decades building a treasure chest of life experiences, would burst at the seams with electrifying and engaging stories—especially those related to his combat service during the Second World War.

I remain somewhat uncertain as to the path that actually led me to Gerling or how we were first introduced, but since I frequently interview veterans for a weekly column printed in local newspapers and a military historical website, my goal has always been to prioritize my visits with World War II veterans. The reason for this is that common sense and statistics dictate we are losing these national treasures at an alarming rate and in a few short years, all firsthand accounts of this war will be lost from us. To be able to capture and preserve their stories in a direct, as *experienced-in-the-flesh* format, it has become my *modus operandi* to move WWII veterans to the top of my interview list while we still have the benefit of learning from them in a first-person context. Obviously, to have made the connection to a veteran with Gerling's background was truly a fortuitous and unexpected gift ... and one that I certainly was not going to let pass me by so easily.

Although I have previously published compilations that presented the experiences of dozens of our local veterans through brief vignettes and photographs, admittedly, it was not my initial objective to collect Gerling's experiences for placement into a book. During the time I spent building these collections of veterans' stories, I continued to interview scores of local veterans from various wars and eras; however, when I met Gerling and began to learn of his military experiences, I knew his story was deserving of so much more attention. I quickly realized this was not a story to be condensed into a few dozen paragraphs; instead, I found it merited preservation in a more extensive configuration.

The narratives I used to structure this endeavor come from several newspaper articles that were later adapted and expanded into what has become this book. The initial article I penned, which appeared in the *Jefferson City News Tribune* during the summer of 2014, highlighted Gerling's entry into the U.S. Army and his subsequent placement in the 609th Tank Battalion and unfolded into a general outline of his service both during and after the war. But while we spoke during our first meeting, I learned tidbits of experiences from his time spent in combat, many of these instances which might be appropriate for a follow-up interview—and, consequently, another article.

As I soon discovered, while stationed in Germany as part of the occupational forces after the end of the war in Europe, Gerling stumbled upon a German *Mother's Cross* while "nosing around"- a bombed-out building in Nuremburg after delivering tank destroyers to be shipped in support of the war in the Pacific. This cross, he discovered, possessed its own historical significance (which will be described in later chapters) and had become an item that, as Gerling informed me, he wished to donate to a museum for preservation and so that it could to be shared with others possessing an interest in military history. I agreed to meet with Gerling regarding his acquisition of the cross while also coordinating the donation of the bygone piece to the Cole County Historical Society in Jefferson City, Missouri.

In the days that followed my discussions with Gerling regarding the German medal in his possession, I received word from the French Consulate in Chicago that he had been approved to receive the French Legion of Honor Medal,[1] an accolade for which I had nominated him

---

[1] French Legion of Honor is an order of distinction which is divided into five categories: *Chevalier* (Knight), *Officier* (Officer), *Commandeur* (Commander), *Grand Officier* (Grand Officer) and *Grand Croix* (Grand Cross). The highest degree of the Order of the Legion of Honor is that of Grand Master, which is held by the sitting President of the

several months previous. While meeting with Gerling to conduct the second interview, I had the unique pleasure of not only sharing with him the details of the significant honor he would soon receive from the French government, but also accepted the German medal for endowment to the local historical society.

After collecting information from the former soldier regarding his discovery of the German medal, I was then able to coordinate the presentation of the French Legion of Honor Medal to be made by Missouri Governor Jay Nixon. Prior to the actual presentation, I penned another article highlighting the donation of the German medal to the Cole County Historical Society, also mentioning that the former tanker was selected to receive the venerated French medal. On January 22, 2015, in his office in the state Capitol, Missouri Governor Jay Nixon presented the award to Gerling during a ceremony attended by a handful of friends and family.

"The drive to liberate Western Europe from Nazi domination came at the cost of many thousands of American lives," Gov. Nixon said during the presentation. "The number of U.S. troops killed or wounded in the Battle of the Bulge, fought in December 1944 and January 1945, was particularly high. That did not stop our soldiers, whose heroism and sacrifice sustained the fight until the Nazis surrendered unconditionally. I am pleased to help honor these Missourians who were part of the Greatest Generation, and who accomplished so much to free millions of people."

While attending this event and witnessing the reverence the governor and elected officials possessed for the services rendered by Gerling and his fellow servicemembers, I began to comprehend fully the depth of the fascinating history experienced by the icon standing before me. This realization soon influenced my decision to return to Gerling's home and interview him about his participation in the rescue of a

---

Republic. The honor was first established by Napoleon Bonaparte in 1802 and may be awarded to American World War II veterans who fought in one of the four campaigns in the liberation of France, which include Normandy, Provence, Ardennnes, and Northern France. Applications for the Legion of Honor are made through one's nearest French consulate. France in the United States, *France Honors American World War Veterans,* http://ambafrance-us.org.

stranded tank in early 1945—an action that earned the former soldier a Bronze Star Medal for valor. All of this, of course, occurred after the battle-hardened veteran had served during one of the deadliest engagements in World War II history- the *Battle of the Bulge*.

This heroic event, when merged with several of the previous stories I had heard the aged veteran recite, soon began to cement my decision to share his exploits in the format of a book. It was also in this timeframe that the movie *Fury* was released in theaters, following a flurry of other popular World War II films in recent years. Though *Fury* provided a rather passionate portrayal of the activities of a Sherman tank crew in the waning days of World War II, watching such a film truly paled in comparison to an actual opportunity to visit with a man who had experienced many similar events firsthand, and thus imbued me with a sense of obligation to share his story.

For nearly two years, I had the honor of conducting personal interviews and enjoying reflective conversations with Gerling in the living room of his rural farm home. I not only uncovered a treasure trove of historical insights regarding a man who left his farming community to become part of a unique organization during the Second World War, but also acquired historical insight from the perspective of an enlisted man. Often, military historical insights are written from the perspective of commanding generals and high-ranking officers, but Gerling's captivating experiences are through the eyes of a non-commissioned officer who served his entire time in a tank destroyer battalion, an organization that existed in the U.S. military for just less than five years.

Gerling was one of thousands of soldiers subjected to the orders of generals who arranged grandiose war strategies several echelons above a tank destroyer crews' narrow sphere of influence. Regardless, he and his fellow soldiers did their duties to the best of their abilities and without hesitation, fail or complaint. This book is not intended to summarize or judge combat tactics or strategy, instead, it demonstrates one man's unexpected journey from his rural mid-Missouri home when drafted in 1941 and follows him as he made the journey of more than 1,200 miles across the war-ravaged terrain of Europe, simply answering his nation's call to the colors. This is the unadorned narrative of farmer-turned-soldier who helped respond to the deadly threat of German armor—a simple testament and tribute to the men and women we now call the "Greatest Generation."

Most importantly; however, is the fortune I received by having the opportunity to refer to Staff Sergeant Norbert Gerling by a name that truly expresses the depth of gratitude I have for the sacrifices he has made for our freedoms while also demonstrating the bond we developed in chronicling his time spent overseas during the war. Norbert is not only a hero in my book (quite literally), I am fortunate to have called him a *friend*. God bless you and your service to this nation, Staff Sergeant Gerling and may we never forget the sacrifices made by you and those with whom you served.

Jeremy P. Ämick
Russellville, Missouri
December 2018

Chapter 1

Humble beginnings ...

"If you made a dollar a day, it was a big wage during those times, but a day was day—not just eight hours; it was until the sun set when you were working on a farm." – Norbert Gerling speaking about growing up during the Great Depression.

If there is one thing that was certain about Norbert Gerling, it is the pride he effused when discussing his service within a unique component of the U.S. Army that was created and later disbanded all within the period of the Second World War—the tank destroyer battalions. While serving as a gunner aboard an M-18 Hellcat that was attached to Company C, 609th Tank Destroyer Battalion, Gerling's uniformed

Jeremy Paul Ämick

service carried him hundreds of miles across the battered European landscape. It was an experience, he related, that resulted in many harrowing adventures, one of which earned him a Bronze Star medal for valor and would later serve as the foundation for a distinguished honor bestowed by the French government. His personal combat experiences notwithstanding, it was the moments he discussed the service of fellow veterans that you could witness Gerling's demeanor swing from focused reflection to glowing enthusiasm when given the opportunity to describe their contributions to the war effort, hesitating to draw any attention toward his own activities in the combat zone.

An ideal example of his humility-laden perspective is demonstrated through the manner in which he described his attendance at a ceremony on May 8, 2015, during an event marking the seventieth anniversary of the allied victory in Europe, widely known in military and historical groups as *V-E Day*. (The same event also celebrated the 131st anniversary of the birth of President Harry S. Truman—a Missouri native with the distinction of ending the Second World War.[2]) Held at the Harry S. Truman Library and Museum in Independence, Missouri, the keynote address was given by Brigadier General Bob LeBlanc,[3] one of thousands of soldiers who had served under General Patton in the Second World War and whose contributions to the war effort did not go unnoticed by men such as Gerling.

Born and raised in the state of Louisiana, Robert LeBlanc graduated from Louisiana State University in 1942 (where he participated in the ROTC program) and began his military career when called to active duty later the same year. Though he served in several capacities during World War II, the most notable was his service as a Special Operations liaison officer between General George S. Patton's Third Army and the French underground forces. He later served as a special operations officer when transferred to the China-Burma Theater in 1944 and joined the Louisiana National Guard after the war ended. For the next two decades, LeBlanc continued his military career as a National Guardsman

---

[2] Harry S. Truman Library and Museum, *70th Anniversary of the End of World War II*, www.trumanlibrary.org.

[3] . The Acadian Museum, *Living Legends*, www.acadianmuseum.com.

The Lucky Ones

while also enjoying a full-time career with the United States Postal Service, eventually receiving promotion to Sectional Center Manager/Postmaster for Lafayette where he supervised ninety-three post offices in southwest Louisiana. On March 20, 2018, LeBlanc was "among the surviving members of the World War II-era Office of Strategic Services to be honored Wednesday with a Congressional Gold Medal" during a ceremony held at Emancipation Hall in Washington, D.C.[4]

"As [LeBlanc] described during his speech, he was part of a group of two hundred and seventy-five people who jumped into France several weeks before the invasion [D-Day] and helped organize the French resistance," Gerling excitedly explained, grinning like a young boy who had been granted the opportunity to meet a personal hero. "I had always wondered why things went so smoothly for us when we traveled through France … and now I know that he was part of reason." Gerling added, "I then asked one of the event organizers if there was any way that I could meet him after the event was over and he said that he'd see what he could do."

Gerling soon received the honor of enjoying the general's company while sitting at his table during a luncheon following the ceremony, providing the former tank destroyer with an unanticipated opportunity to "pump the general for information," Gerling said, emitting a sly grin. "He told me that everyone in his group [that parachuted into France] had to be able to read, write and speak French. They weren't in charge of doing any destructive type of

Taken in the mid-to-late 1920s, Gerling (in bib-overalls, standing, center) is pictured is with the following individuals, beginning with the woman to Gerling's right and moving clockwise: Matilda (sister); Anna (mother); Rose (sister), Marcellus Nilges (nephew); Myrna Jones (Gerling's teacher at Teal School); and Martha (sister). *–courtesy of Norbert Gerling*

---

[4] March 20, 2018 edition of the *Acadiana Advocate*.

work; what they did was to organize communication networks and activities such as that."

But for one to appreciate Gerling's modest descriptions of his own service and to fully comprehend the breadth of events to which he was exposed during his time in the tank destroyers, one must first be introduced to the humble beginnings that brought him into military service. His story emerges from rustic upbringings and his keen attention to developing the skills necessary to succeed as the youngest child in a family raised on a small farm situated on the fringes of a rural Missouri county.

"The World War II folks are getting pretty scarce these days," commented Gerling during one of several extensive oral interviews held at his peaceful home near Henley, Missouri, in 2014. The cacophony of chirping birds and crickets that provided the serene soundtrack for his country surroundings was a luxury he was rarely able to enjoy when traveling across Europe inside the bowels of a rumbling tank more than seven decades earlier.

The road leading to the veteran's home possessed features as circuitous and austere as his journeys through Europe: a two-lane blacktop winding its way over a single-lane bridge before crossing a creek, and all the while hugging the boundaries of lush farmland. This journey eventually led to a non-descript exit onto a single-lane gravel road and eventually carried the visitor to his small home overlooking rich fields adjacent to the Osage River.

Born on May 26, 1919, Gerling was the youngest of seven children, growing up with one brother and five sisters. According to the 1930 U.S. Federal Population Census, Gerling's father, Henry, was the son of Micheal Gerling, a

Growing up on a farm, Gerling notes that the cutting of firewood became an integral chore for two reasons—first, for heating of the home, secondly, to provide fuel for the stove his mother used to cook food for the family. *—courtesy of Norbert Gerling*

German immigrant who eventually established himself as a farmer in the St. Thomas community.

"My dad also became a farmer and mom was a homemaker," he said, recounting the details of his home environment as a child. I was born about two-and-a-half miles from here," he said, pointing his index finger in an unknown direction. "Near the town of St. Thomas[5]."

Much of his formative experiences unfolded during the early days of the Great Depression—a period he summarized with the simple, unembellished assertion, "There was just no money then." He added, "If you made a dollar a day, it was a big wage during those times, but a day was a day—not just eight hours; it was until the sun set when you were working on a farm." The family farm, he further illustrated, was central to the continued existence of the rural family and was a place to raise both food and one's children, not what he has seen occur in more recent farming operations where a specific crop grown or livestock raised and a majority of the food purchased from local supermarkets.

The Great Depression was a difficult period for the majority of Americans and presented a host of unique challenges for farmers, including those located in Missouri. From the period of 1930 to 1940, many farmers had to contend with low prices, bad weather conditions and chinch bugs, the latter of which "invaded and destroyed the crops that the farmers had raised."[6] Other challenges that worked against the farmers during this timeframe were wet conditions that prevented farmers from getting their crops planted, drought situations that led to dustbowl conditions in adjoining states, and an infestation of grasshoppers that caused significant damage to the crops.

"Back in those days," he said, "no one went about expecting a big future or to make their fortunes from their farm. Basically everything we needed to survive came from the farm ... in fact, pork and beans was about the only thing I can remember my mom buying in a can," he said. Leaning forward in a worn chair with a few spots of frayed stitching showing, Gerling further noted most of the farms in the surrounding

---

[5] The community of St. Thomas is in the southeastern section of Cole County, Missouri, and, according to the 2010 U.S. Federal Census, boasted a population of 263 people.

[6] Lowe, *Farming in the Great Depression*, http://library.truman.edu/.

area had orchards that would provide a family with peaches, apples and other fruits that were then canned and later used during the non-growing months. Chickens provided a source of meat and eggs for many families in their communities. The butchering of hogs also became an important event within surrounding area as families and friends would gather to help cure the meat since no refrigeration was available to preserve what they viewed as an essential food source.

Raised in the Catholic faith, Gerling attended church in nearby St. Thomas and received his education at a site called Teal School (with the exception of two years of religious training at St. Thomas)—a small, one-room country school which, he explained, was torn down several decades ago following the consolidation of the local school systems. The walk to school in St. Thomas, Gerling noted, was approximately three miles through the woods and required him to take a ferry across the Osage River. Gerling would often stay with his older sister and her husband, Sarah and Herman Nilges, during the week, returning home on Fridays.

Elizabeth Kempker is pictured in the late 1930s. She and Gerling married in 1946 but the couple first had to endure four years of separation necessitated by Gerling's unanticipated military service. *–courtesy of Norbert Gerling*

When reaching the eighth grade, he and many of his friends had arrived at the pinnacle of their formal education, thus necessitating they make a key decision based upon their geographical location and the availability of transportation.

"Eighth grade was pretty much it for us unless you chose to go to high school, but you had to have your own transportation because there weren't any bus routes running back then," he said. "The nearest high school was twelve miles away [in the small community of Eugene], so I stayed home and helped my father on the farm. That's just the way things worked out."

With little employment available in the area, with the exception of "bucking hay bales[7] for a local farmer" during the summer or other forms of associated agrarian work), Gerling spent the next several years assisting his parents on their farm. As they plodded through the Great Depression, other opportunities started to unfold and the young man found employment helping a local carpenter build homes.

During this timeframe, he also began to develop affections for a young woman whom he had met through neighborhood connections, Elizabeth Kempker. Although this young woman would later become his wife, the couple would not embark upon their life of wedded bliss until they first endured four years of being apart. The separation they soon experienced, he explained, was triggered by a letter that came by mail, bringing with it an end to his employment as a carpenter and securing his participation in a profound segment of American military history.

* * *

"My draft letter came in the mail in October [1941]—'We want you!' it said. It was really strange getting a draft notice back then and folks really made a big deal about it because it was two months before Pearl Harbor and the start of the war," Gerling explained. "There were a couple of boys from the St. Thomas area that had gone ahead and volunteered to enlist, but I believe I was the first one from the area that was drafted."

The war in Europe had raged for more than two years before the United States was drawn into the fray. On the morning of December 7, 1941, hundreds of Japanese planes attacked the American naval base at Pearl Harbor near Honolulu, Hawaii. The singular event deprived the base of "air protection and inflicted heavier damage on the United States Navy than had been suffered in all of World War I." The following afternoon, the United States Senate and House of Representatives met at a joint session in the nation's Capital during which President Franklin Roosevelt asked that "Congress declare that since the unprovoked and

---

[7] Bucking hay bales refers to the process of manual labor during which workers pick up square hay bales from a field, "buck" them up onto a wagon that is towed behind a vehicle (generally a tractor), stack the bales and then haul them to a storage a storage facility, such as a barn, to be unloaded and stacked inside.

dastardly attack by Japan on Sunday, December 7, a state of war has existed between the United States and the Japanese Empire." That same afternoon, the Senate and House both adopted resolutions declaring a state of war with Japan, with President Roosevelt signing the declaration at 4:10 p.m.[8]

Prior to the declaration of war, the nation was crafting plans of defense, which resulted in the *Selective Training and Service Act.* The act was instituted in the United States on September 16, 1940 and became the first peacetime draft in the history of the country, requiring men between the ages of twenty-one and forty-five to register. Those who were selected because of the draft lottery were then required to serve a minimum period of one year; however, as Gerling later discovered, certain events necessitated the extension of the term of enlistment for many a draftee. As a result of the act, it is estimated that by the time of war's end in 1945, more than fifty million men had been registered and ten million inducted into the military.[9]

Although initially given a one-year obligation to the U.S. Army due to the draft, Gerling said that when the Japanese attacked Pearly Harbor weeks later, "everything changed," triggering an extension of the duration of Gerling's and his fellow soldiers' commitment to the country from twelve months to the duration of the war.

Arriving at Jefferson Barracks,[10] (in south St. Louis, Missouri) in early November 1941 for induction into the U.S. Army, Gerling and a group of recruits spent nearly a week on the post, receiving their uniforms, undergoing physical exams and taking aptitude tests, in addition to "killing time because we knew we weren't going to be staying there

---

[8] Miller, *History of World War II*, 310.

[9] The National World War II Museum, *The Draft and World War II*, www.nationalww2museum.org.

[10] Established in 1826 as a permanent military reservation to replace Fort Bellefontaine, Jefferson Barracks served as an induction and separation center, a basic training site and the largest technical training school for the Army Air Corps during World War II. In 1946, the site was considered "excess" and has since that time become home to several National Guard and Reserve units. Jefferson Barracks Community Council, *History of Jefferson Barracks*, http://jbccstl.org.

for long." He and his fellow inductees possessed no idea, he admitted, for what duty assignment or location they were destined.

He soon received orders for Fort Bragg, North Carolina to begin the process of transforming from farmer to soldier through basic training, arriving at the military post in the latter days of November. Named for Confederate general and native North Carolinian Braxton Bragg, Camp Bragg was established on September 4, 1918 and was re-designated "Fort Bragg" in 1922. During World War II, Camp Bragg became an airborne training center and the population of the post exceeded 100,000 personnel by the middle of 1943. Additionally, "tens of thousands of artillerymen were trained on the post's extensive ranges" during the war, with many of these soldiers later used to populate the tank destroyer units.[11] The twelve-week course that Gerling and many of his fellow trainees went on to complete during their initial training was unexpectedly compressed into eight weeks when the Japanese attacked Pearl Harbor the following month and war was declared against Japan.

"Pearl Harbor really changed everything," he soberly remarked.

Thus began the intriguing story of a man yanked from his quiet rural upbringings and the woman with whom he was in love, and thrust into the preparatory stages of acquiring the skills to survive in the threatening arena of armored opposition on a hostile foreign frontier. A substantial interval would pass before Gerling returned home—months grew into years as he moved between military posts throughout the United States and eventually deployed to Europe in support of the war. However, the frenetic events that would come to define the next few years of his military experience were soldered into his memory and became narratives he could lucidly describe even decades later.

---

[11] Fort Bragg, *Fort Bragg History*, www.bragg.army.mil.

Chapter 2

From the farm to the "Hellcat"

"You never asked questions [as to why] you got a new piece of equipment, you just learned to operate whatever you were given the best that you could." –Norbert Gerling speaking about training with a 75mm gun at Ft. Bragg, North Carolina, in 1942.

Gerling and the men with whom he would spend nearly the next four years finished their mobilization training program in early January 1942. Although experiencing a condensed training cycle due to the exigencies presented by the Pearl Harbor attack, they had invested a number of hours receiving instruction in standardized subjects to include defense against chemical attacks, interior guard duty, field fortifications and camouflage, map reading, physical training and organization of the Army. Once this was finished, their training group remained at Ft. Bragg and was temporarily placed under the guidance of the Ninth Infantry Division, with whom they would begin to receive specialty training related to serving as tank destroyers. However, as Gerling and his fellow soldiers were soon advised, they were slated to become part of a formation that would develop into one of the most renowned groups to emerge from the annals of World War II tank history—the 609th Tank Destroyer Battalion.

Officially, the organization was activated on December 15, 1941 at Ft. Bragg and consisted of a headquarters and headquarters company with a medical detachment, three tank destroyer companies and a pioneer company.[12] As Gerling further noted during his interview, the 609th was populated primarily from soldiers in the Ninth Infantry Division with fillers for the battalion coming from the Field Artillery Replacement Center. As Gerling modestly described, tank destroyers were individual battalions "attached to a bigger outfit" and would often "go in when somebody needed some help"—a lesson he would experience firsthand two years later.

The tank destroyer battalions were a concept born in response to threats that had been identified in conflicts unfolding after the First World War, during which the ineffectiveness of anti-tank guns against armored threats had been realized—one notable example being the German invasion of Poland in 1939 and the defeat of the French Army in 1940. With the rise of the German Panzer divisions, the U.S. Army "came up with its own solution ... a

Pictured is the tank destroyer emblem, showing a black panther gripping tank tracks in its teeth. The motto "Seek, Strike, Destroy" was coined by General Andrew D. Bruce. (Public Domain)

---

[12] *A Mini History of the 609th Tank Destroyer Battalion*, Ahrenholz, 1.

The Lucky Ones

semi-independent combat army deployed specifically to deal with the panzer threat."[13]

As noted in *FM-18-5: Organization and Tactics of Tank Destroyer Units* (approved June 16, 1942), the general organization of the tank destroyer battalion consisted of a headquarters and headquarters company, three tank destroyer companies and a reconnaissance company. Each individual tank destroyer company was comprised of a headquarters, one light destroyer platoon, and two heavy destroyer platoons. In essence, the field manual further explains, the tank destroyers' primary role was to serve as an "offensive action against hostile forces" and be capable of "… semi-independent action but preferably operate in close cooperation with friendly units of all arms." [14]

A tank destroyer center was established at Ft. Hood, Texas in late 1941 and headed by General Andrew D. Bruce, a combat veteran of the First World War who later in his career served in the War Department. Bruce was born in St. Louis, Missouri, but grew up in Texas and went on to have a storied military career beginning with his entry into the Army as a second lieutenant in 1917. A graduate of the Agricultural and Mechanical College of Texas (now Texas A&M University), Bruce returned from combat service in France having risen to the rank of lieutenant colonel and serving in many capacities prior to World War II, including the instruction of military tactics, tours of duty at the Infantry School and foreign service in Panama, historical work at the Army War College and military doctrine duties with the War Department. After organizing and commanding the Tank Destroyer Center at Ft. Hood in the early 1940s, Bruce commanded troops of the 77th Infantry in several World War II campaigns in the Pacific. The general later commanded the Seventh Division in Korea and filled several staff positions until his retirement in 1954, at which time he became the president of the University of Houston. Two years later, the former Army general became the school's first chancellor. The recipient of several distinguished decorations and medals including the Distinguished Service

---

[13] Zalgoa, *US Tank and Tank Destroyer Battalions*, 5.

[14] Archives.org, *FM 18-5*, www.archives.org.

Jeremy Paul Ämick

Cross, Distinguished Service Medal with Oak Leaf Cluster, Navy Distinguished Service Medal, Legion of Merit, Bronze Star and the Purple Heart, General Bruce passed away on July 28, 1969 and is buried in Arlington National Cemetery.[15]

Under his leadership and guidance (and later through sometimes heated debates with General Lesley J. McNair[16]), General Bruce is recognized as having played a major role in the development of the tank destroyers in their transition from towed guns to self-propelled weapons. Furthermore, he is attributed with having coined the organization's motto of "Seek, Strike, Destroy," which emphasized the need for an armor component that could "rush to the scene at high speed and destroy the panzers in a fast-moving battle of maneuver."[17]

Those selected to serve in the tank destroyer battalions were soldiers provided with a clear set of expectation and who were to possess specific fighting characteristics and a sense of teamwork to underscore their success under the threats of deadly enemy armor. As noted in the *Tank Destroyer Field Manual: Organization and Tactics of Tank Destroyer Units (FM 18-5)* published in 1942, "Tank destroyers are taught that they must be superior soldiers. The moral qualities of aggressiveness, group spirit, and pride in an arduous and dangerous combat mission must pervade each tank destroyer unit. All ranks must possess a high sense of duty, an outstanding degree of discipline, a feeling of mutual loyalty and confidence with regard to their comrades and leaders, and a conscious pride in their organization."[18]

---

[15] Kleiner, *Andrew Davis Bruce*, http://www.tshaonline.org.

[16] Lieutenant Lesley McNair, who at the time was serving as commander of the Army Ground Forces, often objected to General Bruce's opinion as to the type of tank destroyers needed by the Army's ground forces. Green, *American Tanks*, 208. A native of Verndale, Minnesota, McNair was killed shortly after D-Day in 1944 when the Army Air Corps accidentally dropped bombs on his position in St. Lo, France, while observing the Army's push into mainland Europe during *Operation Cobra*. Lieutenant General McNair is possibly the highest-ranking officer to have been killed during the war. Sadly, two weeks later, McNair's son was killed by a sniper while serving in Guam.

[17] Zalgoa, *US Tank and Tank Destroyer Battalions*, 13. Verndale, Minnesota, Gen. Lesley J. McNair, www.verndalemn.com.

[18] Tank Destroyer Field Manual, *Moral Qualities*, 8.

The Lucky Ones

A gun crew operates an M3 37mm anti-tank gun at Camp Carson, Colorado. Gerling learned to operate a similar weapon while in training at Fort Bragg, North Carolina from December 1941 through January 1943. –*NARA*

Although several tank battalions began to see action in the Mediterranean theater toward the latter part of 1942, Gerling remained at Ft. Bragg and was eventually assigned as a crewmember with Company C, 609th Tank Destroyer Battalion. The company, the young soldier discovered, would remain at Fort Bragg to continue their training for combat by not only undergoing basic military skills refinement—such as small arms firing, physical conditioning, etc.—but also learning to operate anti-tank pieces that included the towed 37mm gun. Manufactured by Watervliet Arsenal, New York, with a carriage being built by Rock Island Arsenal in Illinois, the M3 37mm Anti-Tank (AT) Gun was designed using a German 37mm gun as a template and was able to be towed by a Jeep or truck. When detached from a vehicle, the gun could be maneuvered into firing position by the crew. Though it would often prove effective in piercing and disabling enemy tanks, the M3 possessed certain protective limitations such as "her rather smallish shield meant to protect the crew against incoming enemy fire." The AT Gun was phased out of service shortly after the end of World War II, although in some instances other armies used it in a frontline capacity until 1970.[19]

"The 37mm became the very first gun we trained with when we organized the 609th," Gerling explained. "We actually didn't use it for too long, if I remember correctly, because we later got halftracks with a 75mm gun mounted on them. The 37mm was actually a little light and really the only way it would be effective was if you were able to knock the track off of a tank ... it was just too light a caliber."

---

[19] MilitaryFactory.com, M3 *37mm AT*, www.militaryfactory.com.

15

Another early version of the tank destroyer, the 75mm to which Gerling referred was the M3 Gun Motor Carriage Half-track Tank Destroyer. The vehicle had a crew of five, which consisted of a commander, driver, gunner and two ammunition handlers, and could reach forty-three miles per hour on roads with an average driving range of two hundred miles. As part of the gunnery crew, Gerling would have been somewhat exposed in the half-track since he operated in the rear, open-air section of the hull.[20] Gerling also explained that although the half-track was a "pretty rough ol' thing," when describing the vehicle's suspension, it was also very maneuverable and would "almost climb a mountain."

He further noted, "From the very first day I began training with the 609th, I was assigned as a gunner ... that's all I ever did. You never asked questions [as to why] you got a new piece of equipment, you just learned to operate whatever you were given the best that you could."

As the war continued to unfold, many companies sought ways to demonstrate their patriotism while also supporting those serving on the home front and overseas in combat zones. For Gerling's fellow Missourian, the famed Walt Disney, patronage came in the form of the creation of military insignias utilizing cartoon characters and the talent of the company's artists. Establishing a specialized "unit devoted to producing customized military insignias free of charge for U.S. armed forces and their allies,"[21] Walt Disney and his team of cartoonists strived to accommodate all requests they received, which, for the most part, were for Army units and naval vessels. By the

Walt Disney produced nearly 1,300 distinct military insignias during World War II, including this one for the 609th Tank Destroyer Battalion. It features a tiger cub in a helmet preparing to knock a tank out of commission. – *courtesy of Norbert Gerling.*

---

[20] MilitaryFactory.com, *M3 Gun Motor Carriage*, www.militaryfactory.com.

[21] Baxter, *When Disney Went to War*, Air & Space Magazine.

end of the war, it is estimated that nearly 1,300 of the distinct insignias had been created.

The 609th Tank Destroyer Battalion received their own special treatment from Disney in early 1942 when they were issued a personalized battalion insignia. The unique design featured a determined tiger cub wearing a helmet and raising his fists in preparation to strike a tank—an action identical to what the M-18 Hellcats tank destroyers of the battalion would later accomplish against the German armor throughout Europe. The insignia was reproduced and, in many cases, painted on the side of the equipment used by the battalion (such as Jeeps, tanks and trucks) throughout the combat theater. Additionally, as with virtually all of the insignias developed by Disney during World War II, the one for the 609th Tank Destroyer Battalion was released as part of a series called "Combat Insignia Stamps" and could be collected by the public. The stamps featured the various military insignias created by Disney and could be gathered in a special album that "provided a space for each stamp with a descriptive paragraph or two giving ... the background and characteristics of the Army, Navy or Marine unit for which the stamp was originally designed."[22]

As the weeks transitioned into months and Gerling remained in training time at Fort Bragg, he found that not all of his time was invested in enhancing the skills that he would later call upon for victory in Europe. Rather, he and his fellow soldiers were given the intermittent opportunity to enjoy a little "down time" at a popular local watering hole called the *Town Pump,* where, on several occasions, the tank destroyers unexpectedly refined their hand-to-hand combat skills in confrontations with fellow trainees who were oftentimes fueled by the noxious mixture of arrogance and alcohol.

Located on the 200 Block of Hay Street in downtown LaFayette, an article in *The Fayetteville Observer* describes the area surrounding the *Town Pump* as "a lively place of movie houses, pool rooms, retail stores and other attractions" that were "just down the road from the barracks and

---

[22] July 11, 1942 edition of the *San Francisco Examiner.*

training fields of Fort Bragg." [23] With the airborne training center also situated on Ft. Bragg, thousands of airborne soldiers were placed in the environment of co-existing with the ground-based artillery troops also on the base, which, in the end, frequently resulted in unfriendly rivalries.

"Oh, I remember the *Town Pump* well," said Gerling. "It was in the heart of Fayetteville and they had an older gentleman in there playing the organ—and of course, they served beer," he grinned. "My unit got into one heck of a fight in that place and almost tore it down—but I wasn't with them when that happened," he interjected. "That really ended up being some brawl and they almost ruined the place." Gerling went on to explain that while stationed at Ft. Bragg, the airborne troops were the first on the base to receive "jump boots," which the tank destroyer crews also received; however, their issuance of the footwear came several months later.

"The airborne guys always kind of felt that they were two or three steps above all the other soldiers on the post because of the training they received and that they could parachute out of airplanes," he remarked. "Our guys went to the bar one evening and some airborne guy told one of our guys take off his jump boots when he came in the door because he hadn't earned the right to wear them ... and that's when it all started!"

Gerling explained that in addition to the training he engaged in during his tenure at Fort Bragg, he was also required to perform several additional tasks. The former soldier is pictured above in 1943 while on guard duty, wearing a .45 caliber pistol. – *courtesy of Norbert Gerling*

During the barroom scuffle that ensued, which Gerling noted became so raucous that it eventually spilled over into the street, one of the members of this battalion was struck in the head with a beer bottle and sustained a slight concussion. Due to the injury, the soldier lost his

---

[23] Roy Parker, Jr., *Hotel's Road to Demolition Would End an Era for the City*, appearing in the April 7, 1991 edition of *The Fayetteville Observer*.

sense of direction and wandered back to the place on Ft. Bragg where they had taken their basic training months earlier.

"Luckily, somebody in the area recognized him and brought him back to our area," Gerling said.

Fifty years later, Gerling discovered the longevity of the memory of the 609th's escapades when attending a company reunion of the battalion held in Fayetteville.

"I got in a shuttle bus to go somewhere and the guy driving saw that I was wearing my 609th hat and asked me I was a part of the group that tore up Fayetteville back during World War II," he beamed. "That brawl must have made some history there!"

***

Gerling's older brother, Hubert, was working on farms in Iowa when he received his notice to register for the draft in early 1941. Norbert and his parents drove to Iowa to pick up Hubert and accompany him to the local draft board in hopes that he would get a better draft number. Ironically, it would be two years before Hubert would receive his official draft notice although his younger brother would receive his only a few months later.

While Norbert was still in training at Ft. Bragg, his older brother, Hubert, was finally drafted and inducted into the U.S. Army Air Forces on October 30, 1942. His discharge papers note that he trained as a teletype operator at Chanute Field, Illinois, and served with the 741st Army Air Force Base Unit during campaigns in both Africa and Italy.

"I think that I recall him talking about serving with an anti-submarine squadron that was

Hubert Gerling is pictured in his U.S. Army Air Forces uniform in 1943. Hubert was drafted while his younger brother Norbert was in training at Ft. Bragg and the two did not again see each other until after the war's end. –*courtesy of Norbert Gerling*

stationed in North Africa," Gerling said, recalling the elder brother he did not again see until after the war's end.

Hubert remained in the Army Air Forces until receiving his discharge at Jefferson Barracks, Missouri, on March 15, 1946, attaining the rank of sergeant and serving more than a year overseas. In the years after the war, Hubert attended the Chillicothe Business College and was employed as an accountant for Mexico (Missouri) Refractories and Kaiser Aluminum. He married his fiancée, Agnes Huhman, on June 29, 1946 in Wardsville, Missouri, and the couple went on to raise two sons and three daughters. The veteran passed away on January 18, 2003 at the Missouri Veterans Home in Mexico, Missouri.

***

Battalion histories describe the addition of junior officers to the 609th Tank Destroyer Battalion with the majority arriving from the Artillery School located at Fort Sill, Oklahoma. In January 1943, the battalion packed up their meager belongings and made their move to Camp Hood, Texas—the site that would serve as their home for the next three months, and where Gerling and his fellow soldiers began to hone their targeting skills through live fire exercises and various types of combat-focused training. Named for United States and Confederate States Army officer, General John Bell Hood, Camp Hood, Texas was officially established on September 18, 1942 near the community

While training at Fort Bragg, North Carolina in January 1942, Gerling enjoyed jovial moment while using his strength to balance three of his friends. Standing to Gerling's left is William "Lacey" Bayless, who went on to serve as a sergeant in command of another tank in Company C; the man on Gerling's shoulders is Phillip Sherman, who delivered fuel to Company C's tanks in Europe; and, on top, Robert Maher, who was later assigned to company headquarters. –*courtesy of Norbert Gerling*

The Lucky Ones

of Killeen, becoming a tank destroyer tactical and firing center with the 893rd Tank Destroyer Battalion as the first major unit to call the post home. When troops began to arrive for armored training, three hundred farming and ranch families had to relocate from the area so that their property could be used to support the expansive training mission of the tank destroyer and armored forces. The camp was designated Fort Hood by 1950 and is one of the largest military installations in the world, comprised of 218,000 acres. [24]

"There was one obstacle course they put us through at Camp Hood that had barbed wire stretched about waist high and we had to maneuver under it. While we were doing that, they had some guns set up with live ammo that they would fire over the top of the wire while we were crawling under it. That was quite an experience!" Gerling proudly exclaimed.

Even with the excitement of all of the training they were receiving in preparation for the inevitable deployment to Europe, Gerling recalled there were a few soldiers who were unable to find the means by which to cope with the stress of their new training environment. One of his fellow soldiers, he explained, was performing what they considered routine guard duty while armed with a pistol; sadly, he took his own life with the weapon for reasons unknown to Gerling and the rest of the battalion.

"I've always been quite a healthy guy, but I never really felt very good the entire time we were in Texas," the veteran sagely stated. "I don't know if it was the dust or the weather, but I was ready to get out of there."

The battalion departed Texas for maneuvers in

The M-18 Hellcat Tank Destroyer had a top range of nearly 60 miles per hour and was armed with a 76mm cannon and a .50 caliber machine gun. It was not designed to confront German armor one-one-one; instead, it was designed to ambush German tanks and disappear, taking advantage of its greater maneuverability. –*NARA*

---

[24] Briuer, *Ft. Hood,* https://tshaonline.org.

Louisiana in April 1943, spending "a couple of months in the woods" performing additional firing drills and scouting maneuvers. These exercises, he explained, required the soldiers to learn to dismount from their equipment and operate on foot, with the potential of placing them "a mile into enemy territory while carrying no identification, memorizing our mission assignments and taking mental notes of our surroundings in case we were captured and later escaped." He added, "There would be no papers or notes on us to show what we were doing there."

While in Louisiana performing scouting exercises and participating "in simulations of everything we might encounter in war time," Gerling noted that the battalion expended large amounts of ammunition to ensure they were prepared for any armored threats they might encounter when arriving overseas.

"I've always said that I cost the government an awful lot of money on those firing ranges," he laughed. "I don't think there was another outfit in all the Army that received as good of training as we did." The battalion then left for their final stateside training location at Camp Shelby, Mississippi, which was established in 1917 and is located twelve miles south of the community of Hattiesburg in the southern section of the state. During the First World War, the camp served as a mobilization support site and since then has been used for training by both active and reserve components of the military. During World War II, Camp Shelby had more than 1,000 square miles dedicated for military training, storage, and mobilization purposes while also housing a prisoner of war camp for German prisoners captured from Rommel's Afrika Korps. In addition to housing units of the Women's Army Corp, the camp helped provide training for several divisions and battalions during the course of the Second World War, including tank destroyers. Currently the largest state-owned training site in the nation, more than 100,000 troops train at the site annually as the camp encompasses more than 134,000 acres, serving as a training ground for the M1 Abrams Tank, Bradley Fighting Vehicles and M109A6 Paladin Howitzers.[25] It was while the 609th Tank Destroyer Battalion was stationed at Camp

---

[25] MiltaryBases.com, *Camp Shelby*, www.militarybases.com

Shelby, Gerling recalled, that they were introduced to the piece of equipment they would operate under combat conditions in Europe—the M-18 Hellcat.

"At that point, it was like going from a Model T to a Cadillac," he grinned, adding, "because it was much faster, more maneuverable and had a better gun than what we had worked with before."

The M18 was "viewed by the US Army's Tank Destroyer command as the ideal tank hunter—fast, hard-hitting, and maneuverable," also operating as the "fastest tracked armored vehicle of World War II, capable of road speeds up to 60 miles per hour."[26] However, many tank destroyers discovered that speed could not make up for firepower as the 76mm gun on the M-18 often proved inadequate against the superior armor of the German Panther and Tiger tanks. When actually employed in combat scenarios in Europe, the tank was often used in the role of fire support for infantry units rather than used to engage enemy armor in an anti-tank capacity.

Gerling takes a moment from his training to pose for a photograph in front of the M-18 Hellcat he used in training while stationed at Camp Shelby, Mississippi. *–courtesy of Norbert Gerling*

As illustrated in the book *No Greater Valor*, many of M-18s were used in more of an offensive capacity and would "race ahead to ambush German armor and then run away before the German tanks could return fire," or, as known in military lexicon, to "shoot and scoot." [27]

The M18 76mm GMC (the official military reference for the M-18) was the result of improvements and refinements of earlier tank destroyer designs that included modifications resulting in much faster speeds and greater armament. The destroyer was equipped with a 76mm main gun barrel and was also armed with a .50 caliber Browning machine

---

[26] Zaloga, *M18 Hellcat Tank Destroyer* 1943-1947, 3.

[27] Corsi, No Greater Valor, 125.

gun. With a maximum driving range of approximately 150 miles, the Hellcat consumed one gallon of gas for each mile of ground covered.

"There was a crew of five for the tank with three in the turret—the tank commander, gunner and loader—and then you had a driver and an assistant driver," Gerling said. "The loader had to be a little fella because he didn't have much room to move around." He continued, "I could rotate my gun in a complete circle in sixteen seconds," said Gerling, when describing the Hellcat's turret traverse system. "Time was critical for us and we depended on speed and accuracy. Everything in the tank was electric over hydraulic and I had a stick for operating the main turret, just like a pistol grip," he said. "Whenever I went in one direction with the stick, the gun went in that direction also."

According to Gerling, his head would fit into the tank's telescopic sights—a type of rubber-lined mask that allowed him see through the M-18's "10-power scope with wide vision"; and, once he was sighted in on a target, an electric mechanism was depressed with his right foot to fire the 76mm gun.

"The first command you gave when you spotted a target was to give the position—'Left rear! Right rear! Front!'" Gerling barked, recalling his past duties when operating inside the tight bowels of a Hellcat. "Even a second or two could mean a lot to us."

In addition to the "regular Army routine," as Gerling described his time spent at Camp Shelby, the battalion continued to familiarize itself with all the functions of the Hellcat, even participating in "friendly contests" to prove who could carry the bragging rights as being the best gunner in the battalion.

"We had this one contest to see who could shoot the best," he said. "There were two teams; each team had four tanks participating [for a total of eight tanks in the contest]. We all were situated on the top of a hill with a small target that moved back and forth on a type of railroad track below us ... but you couldn't see the track [and therefore couldn't predict the direction in which the target would move]." He went on to explain, "The exercise was designed to help us learn how to hit a moving tank and each tank fired ten rounds—forty rounds for each team—to see who could get the highest score. The other team fired first and hit thirty-nine out of forty targets."

Such an initial performance by the opposing team might prove daunting to most; but Gerling and his fellow tank destroyers had in previous months immersed themselves in their training and were by no means intimidated by the task before them. When it came time to demonstrate their proficiency, they fired at the targets and emerged from the contest as victors.

"We [Company C] hit forty out of forty targets," he proudly beamed.

The battalion remained focused on focused preparations for combat maneuvers in the European Theater of Operations; however, not all of their time was invested in refining their tactical skillsets. While in Mississippi, Gerling continued to grow in affections for his love back home and wrote his dear Elizabeth at every opportunity he could find; and, he coyly noted, finally arrived at the decision that he should request her hand in marriage.

"Well, there was a time when me and some of the boys were shooting craps one evening and I ended up winning a bunch of money," Gerling grinned. "I think it was $120 or so, and before I had a chance to spend it all or lose it shooting craps, I took it over to Hattiesburg [Mississippi] and bought a wedding ring."

His intentions may have been centered on entering into wedded bliss with Elizabeth, yet the fulfillment of their commitment to one another would have to wait until after the end of the war.

"With everything going on back then, we didn't want to rush into marriage because you didn't know if you might get killed," he somberly recalled. "It was a situation where you didn't want to

Gerling and his fellow soldiers of the battalion traveled overseas aboard the *USS Hermitage*—an Italian luxury liner converted to serve as a troop transport ship for the U.S. Navy during World War II. The ship had accommodations for more than 6,100 personnel –*NARA*

Jeremy Paul Ämick

create a hardship on a wife back home because back then there just weren't the benefits there are now for the survivors."

With their training behind them, the 609th boarded a train bound for Camp Shanks, New York[28], arriving in early August 1944 at the site that would serve as their overseas deployment staging area. The equipment they had trained with in the previous months, Gerling said, remained at Camp Shelby, since new equipment awaited them at their overseas destination. For the few days they remained in port preparing for departure, Gerling affirmed he retained an eagerness to board a vessel and cross the seas, if only to escape the torture of repetitive melodies.

"Every day," he said, shaking his head back and forth, "there was a Scottish band that played—they had the kilts on and everything. They would march down the streets with bagpipes blaring and playing the same song over and over again. We really got tired of hearing that." Pausing, with a sly grin, he added, "I can still hear that song playing in my head."

On August 10, 1944, with the entire 609th Tank Destroy Battalion aboard the *USS Hermitage*,[29] Gerling and his fellow soldiers began the first leg of their journey bound for the war raging in France.

Battalion histories note that the time the 609th spent on the ship was less than favorable, if not torturous, since most of the air conditioning aboard the vessel was not functioning, making the temperatures in the lower decks "hot as Hades." Gerling recalled that he was fortunate to have been one of the last of the soldiers to arrive on board and was

---

[28] When Camp Shanks opened in 1942, it "contained 1,500 barracks, mess halls, theaters, a hospital, and other buildings where some 1.5 million G.I.s (approximately 40,000 a month) were issued combat equipment and underwent final inspections before shipping overseas." It soon became the largest point of embarkation for troops heading to the European and North African theaters and earned the designation of "Last Stop, U.S.A." Hudson River Valley National Heritage Area, *Camp Shanks World War II Museum*, www.hudsonrivervalley.com.

[29] The *USS Hermitage (AP-54)* was first launched in 1925 as an Italian luxury liner named *SS Conte Biancamano*, but came under the control of the United States Navy during World War II and was converted to operate as a troop transport vessel. The ship was decommissioned and struck from the US Naval registry in 1946, returned to the Italian government two years later and was scrapped in Italy in 1960. NavSource Online, *USS Hermitage*, www.navsource.org.

The Lucky Ones

bunked on the outside area of one of the upper decks. This sleeping arrangement gave him the perception that he could "roll right out of my bunk and right into the ocean;" however, it provided him with freedom from the heat that permeated the interior of the ship and granted the enjoyment of an occasional breeze.

Food during their journey was in limited supply and the soldiers aboard were given only two meals a day, but Gerling proudly described an unexpected benefit he received by virtue of having trained as a gunner in the battalion.

"On our trip across the ocean, the ship was short of crew and I got the opportunity to go up on the main deck and help the sailors man one of the guns—a 76mm that was almost identical to the ones we used on the tanks," he said. "When I was working with the gun crew," he paused, his lips shifting into a grin, "I got a sandwich and a second cup of coffee … and we sure appreciated that."

Traveling as part of a convoy, the *Hermitage* arrived in Wales on August 24, 1944, [30]packed to the seams with a battalion of well-trained men lacking indication or hint as to the next leg of movement in their drive toward the battlefield. The journey across the ocean, little did they realize at the time, had been a pause to enjoy since they would soon become participants in a breakneck race across the dangerous and unforgiving European landscape.

---

[30] As noted on Norbert Gerling's *Enlisted Record and Report of Separation*.

Chapter 3

The War in Europe

U.S. Army photograph

"Then he looked at us and said, 'Always let your conscience be your guide in everything you do.' That's something that has always stuck with me." – Words of advice given to Norbert Gerling by his company commander, Captain Stephen Chorak, when crossing the English Channel in September 1944.

Shortly upon their arrival in Wales, the 609th Tank Destroyer Battalion loaded onto several railcars and made the seemingly never-ending journey to Llanover Park Camp located near Abergavenny, Wales, which would serve as their home for the next three weeks. Prior to the arrival of the 609th Tank Destroyer Battalion, Llanover Park Camp was used by American troops for training in preparation for the D-Day landings on Utah Beach, culminating with the first landing of June 6, 1944. Following D-Day, the camp was also used to house

Jeremy Paul Ämick

German and Italian prisoners of war from 1944 until 1946. The camp was part of an old estate belonging to the late Lord Llanover, whose widow donated the use of the land for the housing of troops after the outbreak of World War II. Stables and servant quarters existing on the property were in livable conditions and used by upper-level officers and staff while the remainder of personnel were often quartered in Nissen huts (pre-fabricated structure often made with a skin of corrugated steel and fashioned in a half-cylindrical shape) in other sections of the estate.[31]

While stationed at the camp, the battalion underwent the tedious and labor-intensive processes of preparing for combat by receiving all of their equipment from various depots where it had been stored—including their new M-18 Hellcats. While in the staging area, gunner's such as Gerling worked diligently to ensure the 76mm guns on the tank destroyers were functioning within recognized parameters, a process that also required the soldiers to remove all of the cosmoline from the equipment—a preservative and rust preventative that had been used during the packing and shipment process.

The preparation cycle—much like the training cycle they had experienced at Fort Bragg and previous locations—did afford the men of the battalion a few welcome moments of recreational time, usually resulting in the energetic pursuit of some "spirits."

"There were buses around the camp that made runs into town

The above photograph is of the Red Ball Express as it appeared in 1944. The 609th traveled along part of the legendary route while traveling east toward Metz. The 2-1/2-ton six-wheel-drive General Motors trucks pictured above, often referred to as a "Jimmy" or a "deuce-and-a-half," would operate 24 hours a day delivering supplies to Allied forces.
– *United States Army photograph*

---

[31] After Action Reports, *284th Field Artillery Battalion in World War II*, http://284thfabn.com/helpmate.pdf.

The Lucky Ones

about every night so that a person could visit the pubs if they liked ... because Americans have to have their beer," he smirked. "But I do remember that almost every evening we were under blackout conditions, so the only lights at night were those inside the buildings."

Many communities in European countries in addition to the United States utilized the practice of blackouts during wartime. In coastal regions, blackouts were used to prevent the silhouette of friendly ships being seen from enemy vessels operating at further distances. In other areas, blackouts were used to help prevent against enemy aircraft having the ability to navigate to their intended targets by using sight only. The benefits derived from a blackout have essentially been erased with the development of technological advances such as guided missile systems and night-vision equipment.

Toward the latter part of September 1944, the battalion began their movement across the English countryside, bound for the port that would days later become their debarkation point. The site of their pending departure, Gerling explained, would be their jumping-off point to the location of the famed D-Day landings that occurred only a few weeks earlier. The journey, which took the battalion several days to complete and was an "overland trip of 140 miles" must certainly have been an interesting sight to witness.[32] Resembling a lengthy, steel-laden caravan comprised of all of their equipment including the Hellcats, halftracks, tanks, jeeps and other associated vehicles, the 609th's movement resulted in occasional damage to English property that, Gerling recalls, was attributable to some unanticipated infrastructure limitations.

"Some of the streets were so darn narrow that the tracks of our tanks would scrape the curbs and knock lose chunks of the concrete. Why we went through the towns and didn't find a path around them I'll never know, but we didn't ask questions, we just went where we were told ... when we were told."

Despite any early setbacks in their journey to the debarkation site, the battalion arrived at Weymouth/Portland, where they set about the task of loading LST's—landing ship tanks—for movement to Utah

---

[32] Ahrenholz, *A Mini History*, 8

Beach and their entry into a French countryside now teeming with German opposition. At the time, the battalion had a complement of thirty-three officers, two warrant officers and more than six hundred enlisted men. The LST's they were preparing to board were an integral component of the D-Day invasion as they provided the Allied forces with the capabilities to land heavy equipment in the absence of adequate harbor facilities. Some LST's had the capability to transport as much as 2,100 tons of material, which is equivalent to roughly twenty tanks or four hundred equipped soldiers.[33]

"While we were crossing [the English Channel], our company commander, Captain (Stephen) Chorak, was sitting on the front of one of the tanks. He looked at us and said, 'A lot of you guys have as much or more experience than I do, and when you get off of this LST, you're number one—you should always protect yourself first.'" Pausing in reflection, Gerling added, "Then he looked at us and said, 'Always let your conscience be your guide in everything you do.' That's something that has always stuck with me."

Stephen Paul Chorak was born on September 27, 1917 in Mt. Shasta, California and later graduated from the University of California at Davis. During the Second World War, he served in the European Theater from 1941 to 1945, commanding Company C, 609th Tank Destroyer Battalion under the 10th Armored Division and attaining the rank of captain. In the years following his return home from combat, Chorak was employed for many years by a marketing association and was later worked as a controller with the Tejon Ranch Company. He passed away on November 9, 2005, survived by his wife and son.[34]

In the months following their entry onto the shores of France, Gerling recalled witnessing Captain Chorak's composure in combat, describing him as a "quiet fella that didn't say much because he was always thinking," but a good military man who genuinely cared about the welfare of the soldiers under his command.

---

[33] Battle of Normandy, *Landing Ship Tank (LST) Mk2*, www.dday-over lord.com.

[34] Find A Grave, *Stephen Paul Chorak*, www.findagrave.com.

The Lucky Ones

"The LST he had crossed the channel aboard was loaded with two M-18s and ten men (five-man crew assigned to each each tank)", Gerling said. Making the journey alongside the young gunner was the group of men assigned to Gerling's tank and with whom he would share close quarters for the next several months—tank commander, Alan Iler; tank driver, Raymond Graybeal; assistant driver, Charlie Kuktis; and shell loader, John Roat, Jr.

When approaching Utah Beach, which was cleared of any obstacles from the famed D-Day landings more than three months earlier, the M-18s were required to disembark in several feet of water because the weight aboard the LST would cause it to "ground out" in the sand. A little more than a mile in length, Utah Beach had been used as an access point for armor during the landings, specifically for organizations such as the 70th Tank Battalion. During these landings, the 70th "lost 16 medium tanks, nine at sea" because of such hazards as the sinking of landing craft carrying the tanks, usually from mine explosions, German anti-tank fire, and becoming trapped in water-shrouded shell craters along the beach.[35]

"Once we got there, we kind of lounged around for a day or so," Gerling said of their arrival, "and we really didn't know what to expect. It was simply a situation where you just had to go from one day to another."

They soon embarked on their journey across France by heading east along major supply routes such as the Red Ball Express—"the legendary military trucking operation in the European Theater of Operations (ETO) in World War II that operated around the clock and supplied the rapidly advancing American armies as they streamed toward Germany." This legendary route stretched from the "beaches of Normandy and the ports of the Cotentin Peninsula, principally Cherbourg, to Paris, 270 miles to the east."[36] By the time the use of the Red Ball Express faded in November 1944, nearly 412,000 ton of supplies—including gasoline,

---

[35] Zalgoa, *US Amphibious Tanks*, 26.

[36] Colley, *The Road to Victory*, xii-xv.

food, oil and ammunition—had been delivered by the countless vehicles that traveled the route.

"When we got into France, we got packages of food that were packed specifically for a crew of five people—each package was meant to last a day," Gerling said. "They were carried aboard the tank so that we would have the necessary provisions during our movements."

Unlike their voyage overseas aboard a troopship, the former tanker explained that food was not a major concern during their time spent in Europe; rather, he added, it was his experience that their supply of sustenance was not only reliable, but oftentimes what they consumed was not always lacking in flavor.

The primary packaging they received—known as C-Rations—was one of several types of foodstuffs issued to military members throughout the war in locations where mess halls and food preparation areas were not readily available or feasible under combat conditions. With C-Rations, as Gerling described, food of various types came in tin cans and was pre-cooked. The tank crews would load their tank destroyers with these provisions when passing depots along their routes, which could later be shared with their fellow soldiers who were experiencing less favorable daily living conditions.

Norbert Gerling took a photograph of this imposing German cross-channel gun somewhere near Utah Beach in late September 1944. Several such guns were placed by the Wermacht (German military) along the French coast and were used to bomb enemy ships in the English Channel in addition to possessing the capability to strike military and civilian targets in the United Kingdom. – *courtesy of Norbert Gerling*

"We were able to store a lot of food on our tanks and actually fed a lot of boys that were hungry. When we passed guys in the infantry, we'd open up a box on the tank and throw them out some C-Rations," he said. "For the soldier that walked his way across Europe, it was a little different for them because the C-Rations were a little bit heavy for them to pack along with all of the other stuff they needed to carry into combat."

Rolling through the French countryside, soldiers never seemed to find anything on which to spend any of their paycheck since the shops along the routes they traveled all seemed to have closed before the war reached their doorsteps. Additionally, even when there seemed to be a dearth of food available for purchase on the local markets, Gerling was occasionally able to satisfy his yearning for eggs, although not of the flavor or variety to which he had grown accustomed to back on his family's farm in Missouri.

"We did have a chance to eat some of the eggs in France," he grinned, adding, "but they were preserved in brine, and, believe it or not, they stayed pretty fair ... but I was still a fried egg type of guy. Little things like that made you appreciate what you had back home."

The battalion arrived in the Metz area during the final week of September 1944 where they received a brash introduction to the logistical concerns plaguing a sizeable Army operating thousands of miles from home. In the weeks preceding their arrival, the Third Army, led by General George S. Patton, moved quickly and ripped into the stalwart German defenses; however, with their run through France consuming an estimated 350,000 gallons of fuel each day, Patton's forces were halted in late September 1945 as they waited for their supply train to catch up. This vexing delay would unfortunately provide the German army with adequate time to shore up their forces operating in and around Metz.

Born on November 11, 1885 in the state of California, George S. Patton was a graduate of the United States Military Academy at West Point and early in his military career led Calvary patrols during General John J. Pershing's expedition to Mexico prior to World War I. During the First World War, Patton became the first officer assigned to the newly developed United States Tank Corps. Throughout the ensuing years, he continued to rise through the ranks and worked in a number of staff positions, until the outbreak of World War II, at which point he led the Seventh Army in its invasion of Sicily and later pushed across France while commanding the Third Army. On December 9, 1945, while commanding the 15th Army in American-occupied Germany, Patton was involved in an automobile accident and died twelve days later because of his injuries. The famed general is buried in Hamm, Luxembourg alongside soldiers who lost their lives during the Battle of the Bulge.

"At the present time our chief difficulty is not the Germans, but gasoline. If they would give me enough gas, I'd go all the way to Berlin," lamented General Patton on August 28, 1944. Three days later, fuel delivery problems brought Patton's drive to a halt.[37]

"We sat at Metz for quite awhile waiting for everything to catch up to us," said Gerling. "We ended up running out of fuel and stayed there waiting for everything to get back into place so we could get moving again."

The battalion soon learned to operate under combat conditions, but in a capacity other than that of the tank destroyer competencies for which they had received much training.

"The Germans held Metz for quite awhile because we didn't have the necessary supplies to capture it," Gerling recalled. "Our role wasn't really as tank destroyers at that point; we were used for indirect fire and converted into an artillery type of role. All of our ammunition was rationed and we were given—I think—five rounds every day, and would use them to fire harassing rounds just to let the Germans know that we were still around. Really, we were kind of first responders—if the field artillery [units] were being attacked, they would call us and we would come to the rescue." He added, "During this time we [the 609th] were so split up and scattered to support different units that we would often go on these missions with only one tank."

The 609th continued to operate with their M-18s during the storming of Metz and throughout the remainder of their combat involvement in Europe; however, several of their fellow tank destroyer battalions—such as the 607th—received the newer M-36 tank destroyers, which possessed the larger 90mm main gun, while performing operations in

---

[37] U.S. Marine Corps, *Bulk Fuel Operations*, 1-1.

and around the fortified city of Metz.[38] The many weeks the battalion spent near Metz provided Gerling and his fellow soldiers with several opportunities to "pull guard duty," which, he illustrated, was teeming with dark and quiet moments that could play tricks with one's mind.

"Everybody was so keyed up with all of the action … the combat going on around us," he said. "If you stood guard duty overnight—and every tank crew pulled their own guard duty—you began to think that you'd see an object, and the longer you watched it, the more it really began to look like it was moving like an enemy soldier. Guard duty was really tough because you didn't move at all—you didn't want to give them a target to shoot at."

With a grin, he continued, "We had one guy, I remember, who shot the hell out of a cedar tree one night. He looked at it long enough and I guess convinced himself that it was a German, but then again, that kind of thing happened more than you know." Laughing, he added, "I'm pretty sure the tree survived the attack just fine."

Injuries were a frequent occurrence with artillery rounds going off in the vicinity of their operations, eventually causing Gerling to personally experience the fright of incurring a wound that could have resulted in much greater consequences. With their tanks being used for harassing fire, several of Company C's Hellcats were often set up in a centralized area. They would then construct foxholes for protection and wait until receiving orders to move to another area of operations. It was during one of these lingering periods that unanticipated rounds fired by the enemy came whistling toward their location.

"The Germans began shelling us and the first one that hit near us happened to be a dud," he said. "I knew the next one wouldn't be and I was in the process of diving toward a foxhole when it hit and exploded. The shell sent all sorts of debris hurtling through the air," with a hunk of dirt striking Gerling in the face and breaking one of his teeth.

"They treated me right there and a few days later I went to an aid station and they pulled the stump of the tooth out." Documentation and records for minor injuries, he explained, generally were not kept and

---

[38] Cross, *Tank Busters*, 26-30.

therefore resulted in many soldiers not receiving Purple Heart medals for combat injuries.[39]

One incident, the veteran recalled, could have met with deadly consequences given the right mixture of circumstances; however, in hindsight, he now reflects upon the experience with a certain amount of mirth and relief.

"While we are at Metz waiting for our next mission, I heard a Jeep that kept racing its motor like someone kept stomping on the gas pedal and revving it up. After awhile, I could tell that it was stuck in the mud, so I grabbed a group of guys and we went down there to try and help him out."

When he arrived at the area of concern, he discovered the Jeep was submerged in the mud with a group of GIs surrounding the vehicle and trying to get it moving once again. Gerling approached the group and got behind one of the men already pushing on the back of the Jeep, shoving with his shoulder to provide a little extra "push."

"I looked up and saw that the guy driving was wearing a German helmet, but none of us really thought anything of it because some of our guys were wearing those helmets all of the time (as a type of war trophy, he explained)."

They succeeded in freeing the vehicle and it let it go on its way, but when Gerling returned to the company area, there came an announcement over the radio warning the battalion to be on the lookout for a German soldier moving about the area in a stolen American Jeep.

"Yep, that was me who helped him, I guess," Gerling said with a smile.

As he went on to explain, the situation near Metz remained relatively stagnant for several weeks until ammunition, fuel and other supplies were restored to a sufficient level to allow for the launch of a suitable offensive against the entrenched German forces.

Finally, with a resupplied army and the go-ahead from General Dwight D. Eisenhower, on November 20, 1944, Allied troops under the command of General Patton were able to battle their way into Metz

---

[39] The Purple Heart medal can be awarded to a member of the Armed Forces of the United States, who has been wounded, killed or has died after being wounded.

and begin their drive toward the Siegfried Line and what appeared to be the very doorstep to Germany. The Siegfried Line was often referred to as the "Westwall" during World War II. This defensive line found its roots in the First World War when it was established from a section of a previous defensive line called the Hindenburg Line. The Siegfried Line was more than three hundred and ninety miles in length and consisted of a link of defensive forts and obstacles stretching between Germany's western border, beginning in the north near Kleve in the Netherlands, and moving south to the border separating Germany from Switzerland. Some of the protective measures found along the Siegfried Line included fortified machine-gun outposts known as "pillboxes" and rows of pyramid-shaped concrete blocks known as "dragon's teeth" that were designed to obstruct the movement of tanks and other mechanized vehicles.

Throughout the whirlwind of offenses that followed, the Allied forces achieved several notable advances during the latter months of 1944. While one could submit a litany of overviews and detailed analyses highlighting the various tactical strategies and offensive measures implemented by high level commanders during this period, the enlisted man, the soldier on the ground and operating in mud, likely realized one thing—they were now on the move toward the German border and fighting an enemy not willing to easily relinquish the tactical gains previously won through the blood and sweat of their fallen comrades.

While battles progressed westward, Gerling noted, many of the German countermeasures brought to bear against them have now found a venerated, if not often misunderstood, place in the annals of military history.

"You could hear the V-2 rockets flying over all of the time it seemed," Gerling recalled, "and the 'swishing' sound those mortars made going through the air ... I can still hear them in my mind."

The V-2 rocket was designed under the guidance of famed and influential German rocket scientist Wernher Von Braun, and underwent its first successful testing in October 1942. The weapon eventually became the "first long-range ballistic missile to be actively used in combat" and could hurtle a "1,700-pound warhead 50 miles high and hundreds of miles downrange to its target."[40] Fortunately, the V-2 was introduced too late to deter the Allied forces and to influence the outcome of the war. Despite the threats posed by the V-2s and the array of fatal explosives that often surrounded the American troops, Gerling recalls the presence of an innocuous hazard that became the basis for high levels of discomfort and aggravation among the soldiers with whom he proudly served.

"It seemed to rain a lot over there," Gerling said. "I don't think that I dried off the entire time I was in France," he grinned.

However, as the young gunner would soon discover, the wet conditions they faced would soon transition to bitter cold as they approached Luxembourg in the early part of December 1944. It was during this point in their movement that they were attached to the 10th Armored Division and, unbeknownst to the soldiers of the 609th Tank Destroyer Battalion, were soon to become part of an early response force in one of the most deadly and famous battles in all of America's involvement during the war.

---

[40] Dungan, *V-2: A Combat History of the First Ballistic Missile*, 2-3.

Chapter 4

Recreation

Public Domain

"[The] Sad Sack was a typical GI—just like Beetle Bailey," Gerling beamed. "There always seemed to be one or two guys that acted just like him in every unit in the Army." – Norbert Gerling discussing a cartoon character who provided soldiers many a chuckle during the war.

Jeremy Paul Ämick

On many of the evenings they spent overseas while pushing their way across the French landscape, Gerling and his fellow soldiers gathered around the radio to listen to Nazi propaganda, which, although intended to demoralize the troops serving in Europe, was instead viewed by many of the U.S. soldiers to be both amusing and entertaining.

"We all knew that Axis Sally was part of the German army intelligence, designed to breakdown our morale," Gerling said, describing the radio host that earned a significant level of notoriety during the war.

"Axis Sally" was actually named Mildred Elizabeth Smith (later becoming Mildred Gillars when her mother remarried) and was born on November 29, 1900 in Portland, Maine. She graduated high school from Conneaut, Ohio in 1917 and went on to attend Ohio Wesleyan University with hopes of pursuing a career as an actress. The aspiring performer spent six months completing studies in France in 1929, and later returned to the United States to work as a governess and a salesgirl. In 1935, she moved to Germany, first working as an English instructor but later accepting a job with Radio Berlin as an announcer and an actress. Her radio show was dubbed *Home Sweet Home* and was self-named "Midge at the mike," although the soldiers in the field referred to her as Axis Sally. Broadcasts of her shows could be heard all over Europe, the Mediterranean, North Africa and the United States from December 11, 1941, through May 6, 1945. The former radio host was found guilty for her demoralizing war acts in March 1949, at which time she was sentenced to ten to thirty years imprisonment and a $10,000 fine; however, she would receive parole in 1961 after serving twelve years of her sentence. After her release, Gillars taught at a Roman Catholic school for girls in Columbus, Ohio, and then returned to her old college, Ohio Wesleyan, where she finished the education she had begun decades earlier by earning her bachelor's degree in speech in 1973. Gillars died on June 25, 1988, at the age of eighty-seven.

When [Axis Sally] would come on, the air which was several times a day according to Gerling's memory, the men of the battalion would

The Lucky Ones

gather around to listen to the stories she would tell about the wives, fiancées, and romantic interests of soldiers who were allegedly engaging in unfaithful behaviors back on the home front. In the book *Axis Sally: The American Voice of Nazi Germany*, she was described as "[s]peaking in a breathless voice" and portraying "herself as a much younger but experienced woman. She played the vixen behind the microphone, taunting the men on the front lines and casting doubt in their minds about their mission, their wives and girlfriends, and their prospects after the war."[41]

Gerling said, "I mostly remember listening to her in the evenings and she'd play American music to help entertain you and to get our attention. Then," he continued, "she would read off a list of names of soldiers that were actually serving in the war at that time and tell them that their wife or girlfriend or whatever they had back home was cheating on him with somebody else. Although we knew that it was all a bunch of BS, some of the stories actually sounded like they could actually have been legitimate."

It was also during his extensive journey across the European countryside, Gerling explained, there was a beloved military cartoon character to which he and his fellow soldiers were introduced who provided a steady source of laughs and a little relief from the hardships surrounding them.

"[The] Sad Sack was a typical GI—just like *Beetle Bailey*," Gerling beamed. "There always seemed to be one or two guys that acted just like him in every unit in the Army."

The Sad Sack comic strip made its debut in *Yank, The Army Weekly*—a magazine published by the United States military during World War II—with its first

Sgt. George Baker's popular *The Sad Sack* character was featured on the cover of the first anniversary issue of the Yank magazine in 1943. (Public domain)

---

[41] Lucas, *Axis Sally*, 73.

Jeremy Paul Ämick

publication on June 6, 1942, according to an article found on the U.S. Army's website.[42] The humorous character was "selected as the first permanent feature of the new magazine."[43]

The cartoon was the creation of Sgt. George Baker, a native of Massachusetts who grew up in Illinois and was later hired by Walt Disney Studios in 1937, assisting with the production of animated films such as *Pinocchio, Dumbo* and *Bambi*. Drafted by the U.S. Army in June 1941, five months prior to the attacks on Pearl Harbor, Baker was assigned to the Signal Corps[44] to produce animation for military training films. He grew appalled by the cheerful and tailored manner by which the average soldier was portrayed to the public and embarked upon a personal campaign to depict soldiers in a more authentic manner, resulting in the birth of *The Sad Sack* character.

The fictional comic featured the antics of a clumsy and oftentimes inept soldier of the U.S. Army, who was usually involved in absurd and outrageous situations, inadvertently distressing sergeants and officers within his unit. As Gerling noted, although he enjoyed the photographs and articles in *Yank, The Sad Sack* strip was for him the magazine's focal point.

"Whenever mail call would come, the magazine often came with it," Gerling explained, recalling reading the publication while in Europe several decades ago. "Sometimes GI's would pass them along to each other, and whenever you found one, you read it and then handed it on to someone else to enjoy." Gerling added, "[*The Sad Sack*] was a typical, run-down soldier who seemed to stumble his way into trouble. The humor was great and everybody got a kick out of it … it was something that took our minds off the combat and gave us a little relief from our daily activities."

---

[42] Foster, 'Yank' magazine energized Soldiers, www.us.army.mil.

[43] Baker, *The Sad Sack*, Introduction.

[44] The Signal Corps is the branch of the U.S. Army that develops, tests, implements and manages the communications systems and networks. During World War II, one of the primary functions of the Signal Corps was to train radio operators, who became integral to the success of the many beach landings that occurred during the course of the war.

St. Thomas area veteran and a friend of Gerling's, the late Raymond Herigon, landed on the beaches of Normandy, France, on June 9, 1944 and fought his way across France, Germany, Holland and Luxembourg with the Fourth Infantry Division. Herigon recalled several details of the iconic comic strip, having also served in uniform with soldiers who seemed to possess characteristics that reminded him of the amusing character.

"We all read [The Sad Sack]; we'd get copies of [Yank] every so often," Herigon said. "There was a guy in our unit who reminded us of him—he was always playing tricks on the officers. The guy could whistle exactly like a German shell coming in and he would hide behind tents and scare the heck out of the officers," he grinned.

But as Herigon went on to explain, comics—and the antics they inspired—were integral in helping everyone forget the horrors of combat, if only for a little while.

"We were always playing tricks on each other ... we had to," Herigon said. "Otherwise we would go nuts."[45]

In the years following the war, Sgt. Baker's creation continued through a briefly lived daily comic strip in newspapers, became a comic book series published by Harvey Publications and eventually served as the inspiration for a motion picture starring Jerry Lewis in 1957. The memory of The Sad Sack may have become a near-forgotten phenomenon, yet the soldiers who fought their way across the frontiers of Western Europe remain grateful for the chuckles provided through the blundering frolics of a cartoon character with whom they often felt personally connected.

"[The] Sad Sack was put out for a reason," Gerling paused, "it was meant to give us a little bit of a lift [in our spirits] ... and sometimes we'd only have one magazine for two or three tank crews, but we'd share them among us. But he truly was a very funny character that

---

[45] Raymond Herigon passed away at ninety-three years of age in Jefferson City, Missouri, on May 20, 2016. The World War II combat veteran received two Bronze Stars and the French Legion of Honor Medal in recognition of his service. He was laid to rest with full military honors in the St. Thomas (Missouri) Cemetery.

provided us with a little entertainment and a few smiles in some very difficult times."

Brief respites from combat also came in the form of baseball, a game that held a special place in Gerling's heart from the time he was only a small boy. In the fall of 1944, his two favorite baseball teams, the St. Louis Browns and the St. Louis Cardinals, were engaged in the World Series. The St. Louis Browns were a franchise that existed from 1902-1953 and was perhaps the worst Major League franchise, losing more than one hundred games a total of eight times and finished last in the American League a total of ten times. However, an article notes that the team "probably owed much of their success in 1944 to depleted wartime rosters across the league …" The Browns moved to Baltimore in 1954 after losing eight straight seasons and became the Baltimore Orioles.[46] The St. Louis Browns' appearance in the World Series of 1944 was an event, Gerling affirmed, not to be missed by the troops in field regardless of their combat duties and daily work assignments.

"We were somewhere in the middle of France and somebody had rigged up a radio so that we could listen to the World Series," he said. "We would sit around at 11:00 o'clock at night, I believe, and listen to those games. I had always been a Cardinals fan, but in those days it seemed like the Browns were winning regularly when they played the Cardinals. So, I decided to bet ten dollars that the Browns would take the series."

The National League Champions, St. Louis Cardinals, won the series by taking four games out of six … and Gerling's wallet became ten dollars lighter.[47]

---

[46] Baseball Reference, *St. Louis Browns*, www.baseball-reference.com.

[47] Baseball Almanac, *1944 World Series*, www.baseball-almanac.com.

Chapter 5

Battle of the Bulge

U.S. Army photograph

"When the Germans attacked, we were told that Eisenhower called all his generals in, including ours [Patton], and issued orders to get everyone and everything he could up to Luxembourg as quickly as possible." – Gerling discussing their rush to provide assistance during the emergent Battle of the Bulge.

During the early months of his service in Europe, Gerling had been exposed to several facets of warfare by the time the city of Metz fell. At the time, he did not realize the gruesome and intense conflicts yet to come as the German forces grew more desperate in the face of the Allied forces drawing closer to their borders.

The skirmishes and battles in which the 609th Tank Destroyer Battalion had participated in up to this point—and those yet to come—provided many occasions for the tank crews to devise clever modifications for their equipment. A number of these adaptations were born of necessity, such as a cover for their tank that helped provide a level of protection during the frequent mortar attacks they oftentimes had to endure.

"There was a lot of danger for the tank crews, especially whenever we were operating in wooded areas," he explained. "The shells would come in and explode in the trees and would then fragment the limbs, which caused twigs to shower down on us. One time this happened, all of the members of my tank crew were wounded, so we eventually devised a steel cover to set over the open turret on the tank that would give us better protection when things like this happened," he added.

This type of innovation was frequently applied in combat situations and proved in the weeks following December 16, 1944, when Gerling and the soldiers of the battalion became involved in one of the most intense periods of their wartime service. It was on this date that the Germans launched the greatest offensive of the war in Western Europe—the Battle of the Bulge. The Ardennes sector had been viewed by most military officials as a relatively quiet region, and, according to historical records maintained by members of the 609th, was often used by elements of the First Army to "rotate combat units through for rest, refit and rehabilitation. On occasion, it was also used for combat indoctrination of new units." [48]

Though the First Army was holding an extensive defensive line, they had been operating in tandem with elements of the Third and Ninth Armies to push "for the Rhine over difficult terrain, across swollen rivers, and against determined enemy resistance,"[49] while the southern sector of the line was held by the U.S. Army's VIII Corps. When the

---

[48] *A Mini History*, Ahrenholz, 1.

[49] Marshall, *Bastogne: The First Eight Days*, 1.

German offensive commenced, they were able to break through this line and press sixty-five miles into territories that had been held by American forces only hours earlier, aided in their efforts by the element of surprise, two German Panzer armies and twenty-four divisions.[50]

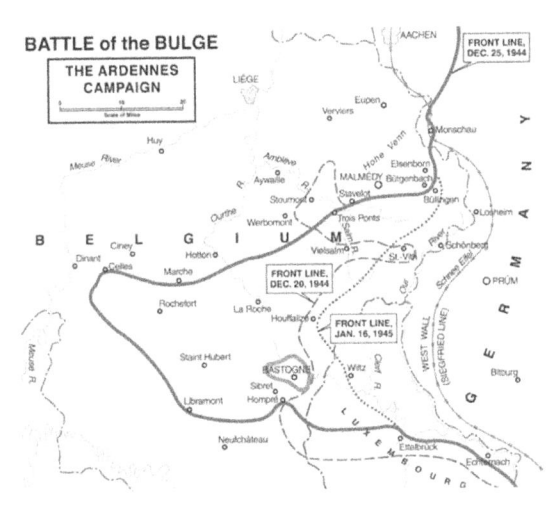

The Battle of the Bulge, also known as the Ardennes Offensive, lasted from December 16, 1944 through January 16, 1945 and not only holds the distinction as being the largest battle ever fought on the Western Front during World War II, but in terms of casualties was the second deadliest battle for the United States military. The German preparation for the offensive, which was codenamed *Wacht am Rhine* (Watch on the Rhine) actually fell short of its offensive goals but created a bulge in the American lines that some historians believe was as deep as sixty-five miles, which, when viewed on a map, would provide the name for this extensive conflict. –*Public Domain*

We were sitting there in position—somewhere in the vicinity of Metz ... just whiling away time, waiting for orders and also for more of our supplies to show up," Gerling remarked. "This gave the Germans enough time to manage to regroup and launch their offensive." He

---

[50] Ambrose, Supreme Commander, 557.

continued, "When the Germans attacked, we were told that Eisenhower called all his generals in, including ours [Patton], and issued orders to get everyone and everything he could up to Luxembourg as quickly as possible."

There were likely scores of rumors and speculation circulating at the time with regard to meetings held in response to the German offensive, but Gerling was correct in that Eisenhower called his senior commanders together on December 19, 1944 at Verdun, France, to discuss the Allied counteroffensive. During this meeting, General Patton "unveiled his scheme to relieve Bastogne," thus resulting in a mobilization of forces that would help "seal his legend as the most aggressive U.S. Army field-commander of the war."[51]

Historical reviews have often concluded that Hitler could have launched a campaign against the Russian forces along the Eastern Front. It was during the war that the Eastern Front became the theater of war between the Axis powers (comprised primarily of Germany, Japan and Italy, along with several smaller, associate nations, and the Allied powers, which included sectors of Northern, Southern, Central and Eastern Europe. This front experienced some of the deadliest battles of the war, which included Nazi Germany's surprise attack on the Soviet Union in June 1941, known as *Operation Barbarossa*—an invasion that included more than three million German soldiers. In the first week of this campaign alone, German forces were able to kill or wound more than 150,000 Russian troops; German forces would eventually suffer more than 700,000 casualties of their own.[52] Despite whatever tactical possibilities could have been exploited along the Eastern Front at that time, Hitler clung to the view that the Western Front offered the greatest opportunity for military success. The Western Front was protected by only a handful of divisions, whereas the Russians had hundreds of divisions that could be brought to bear should a military campaign be launched in the east.

---

[51] ." Zalgoa, *Eisenhower*, 50.

[52] History.com, *8 Things You Should Know*, www.history.com.

The Lucky Ones

The Allies believed—albeit mistakenly, history has demonstrated—that the Ardennes region itself might serve as a deterrent to German incursion. A reason for the area's perceived impenetrability was its steep valleys, ravines and thick forests that created a natural environment of narrow points of entry that made it relatively easy to defend and difficult for enemy tanks to traverse. Within the region, however, some of Hitler's commanders took an interest in a little town on the map by the name of Bastogne, with its seven roads spidering in different directions, thus granting them access to the Allied-held territories in the east and making it a prime strategic objective.

In the book *No Silent Night: The Christmas Battle for Bastogne*, it is noted that along the Western Front, Hitler realized that "the Allies could field a little more than fifteen armored divisions, and just over forty-five infantry and airborne divisions." The author further noted that a sudden attack by German forces comprised of "twenty or more divisions would seriously jeopardize the entire Allied front, particularly if this attack was aimed at a thin sector of the Allied line."[53]

This threatening period remained engrained in Gerling's memories as he recalled being awakened at 9:00 p.m. on the evening of December 16, 1944, when he and the soldiers of his company were ordered to get all of their equipment prepared to move out on a mission. As he explained, his tank crew, as did others with whom he served, often crated makeshift beds under their tanks,

A Sherman tank from the U.S. Army's 37th Tank Battalion of the 4th Division, named *Cobra King*, has "First in Bastogne" written across its side. Both tanks and tank destroyers became critical in providing relief to 101st Airborne Division soldiers who had been encircled by German forces at Bastogne, Belgium in December 1944. *–United States Army photograph*

---

[53] Barron and Cygan, *No Silent Night*, 13.

digging out enough space for four of the men to rest at a time and providing their crews with overhead cover in the event of an artillery attack by the enemy. One member of the crew—the fifth tank crewmember—remained on guard duty to alert those who were sleeping of any emergency that might develop.

"At the time they got us up and told us to get ready to head out, we actually weren't sure of what was going on," he said. "The way everything happened, we thought that the war might be over because they told us to put the lights on the tank, which was something that we normally didn't do because the muzzle blast from the 76 millimeter on the Hellcat would blow the lights out if they were attached when we fired it."

The 609th Tank Destroyer Battalion soon discovered that they were making the journey to the country of Luxembourg, Gerling recalled, to assist in shoring up the defenses in the sectors infiltrated by German forces, with their battalion continuing to operate under the command and control of the 10th Armored Division.

This, as history demonstrates, was the beginnings of the famed Battle of the Bulge, so named for the westward bulging shape of the German incursion into Allied territories as it appeared on a map. Though Hitler's last major offensive would be fought on an eighty-mile front, Gerling's perception of this great conflict was focused on a much smaller sector of the action, specifically, locations in both Luxembourg and Belgium.

Moving north in a battalion formation, Recon Company led the way and were followed by Companies A, B, C, while the formation closed out by the battalion's headquarters company. Company C's first platoon, of which Gerling was still a member, would be delayed in their arrival when some of their tank destroyers were strafed by German aircraft and forced to remain back to await maintenance teams called in to provide the necessary repairs to get them back on their way.

"They hit us about daylight [on December 17th]," said Gerling, recalling the attack by German air assets.

With the rest of the battalion moving forward to enter the Battle of the Bulge, Gerling's platoon was able to return their damaged equipment to operational status within a few days' time and continued their movement to Luxembourg City. Once there, they moved on to the outskirts of Bastogne, yet remained separated from the rest of Company C who were already fighting inside the city. Throughout the next several days, elements of the battalion were shifted around to locations where threats unfolded, while Gerling and crew awaited orders that would marry them up with the rest of the battalion.

* * *

While awaiting further instructions from headquarters, Gerling noted that several platoons within his Company participated in military offenses almost immediately after their arrival in Luxembourg.

"One of our commanders got wind that the Germans were going to take control of a junction where several roads connected in the area," he said, "so he pulled a couple of M-18s from Company C and positioned them on a hill above that location. It was in the morning time on December 20th [1944], I believe, and the fog was so thick and heavy that you couldn't see anything around you, but when it would lift, it was like a window curtain being drawn up," he added.[54]

"The two gunners in the tanks that were sent, Colby Ricker and Justin Double [from Company C's third platoon] said that they just sat there in position, shrouded by the fog, and soon could hear what sounded like tanks idling a short distance away from their position. Then when the fog lifted, they saw a bunch of German tanks sitting at the junction trying to figure out which direction they should go. I heard that in a period of about fifteen minutes, those two gunners of ours were able to knock about fifteen tanks out of service."[55] Official reports note that the tanks destroyed included two types of German Panthers.[56]

In describing the implementation of the early-model Panzers and the later-model Panthers, the latter of which was intended to serve as

---

[54] See *Appendix D* for a report of this incident.

[55] The information Gerling received regarding this incident appears accurate as an official report notes that fourteen tanks were destroyed (see *Appendix D*).

[56] The German Panther—a medium-sized tank that served alongside the heavier Tiger tanks during World War II and is considered by many armor historians to be one of the best tank designs of the war when considering its firepower and armored characteristics.

a replacement for the former later in the war, authors Mike and Gladys Green explain in *Panther: Germany's Quest for Combat Dominance:* "Despite the fact that early model Panzer III and Panzer IV medium tanks were inferior in some design features to their early-war French and British counterparts, such as in armor protection and firepower, the German medium tanks had prevailed over their opponents due to the higher level of training their crews possessed and the tactics those same crews employed in combat."[57] Fortunately for the crews of the Hellcats in the 609th, the training and tactics the American tank destroyers received stateside and during their drive across France prepared them to respond to the greatest of threats that could be offered by their German counterparts.

Born August 8, 1917, Corporal Colby N. Ricker's obituary notes that he was injured during World War II and awarded the Bronze Star and Purple Heart. Cross-referencing through Company C's official records note that Ricker's injury occurred on December 20, 1944, the same date of his participation the offensive against German tanks at the crossroads near Luxembourg. In the years after the war, Ricker returned to his native state of Maine and joined the family business of E.C. Ricker and Son, which sold farm equipment. An active member of his local American Legion and a member of the Disabled American Veterans, Ricker married and became father to three daughters in the years following his return from combat. The veteran passed away in 2007 at the age of eighty-nine and is interred in the Maine Veteran Cemetery in Augusta.[58]

His fellow gunner, Corporal Justin D. Double, was born on May 25, 1919 and raised in Pennsylvania. On October 28, 1941, he entered the service and went on to train alongside Gerling in Company C, 609th Tank Destroyer Battalion in locations such as Camp Hood, Texas and Camp Shelby, Mississippi. Double's biography notes that the event Gerling describes unfolded near the small village of Noville, only a few miles from Bastogne. However, Double's biography goes on to explain that four tanks were involved in the operation; however, two of the M18s were

---

[57] Green, *Panther: Germany's Quest for Combat Dominance*, 9.

[58] The Portland Press Herald, *Obituary for Colby N. Ricker*, http://obituaries.pressherald.com.

The Lucky Ones

in a fixed firing position while the other two destroyers moved through the town. When the fog lifted, Double's destroyer was able to knock out seven enemy tanks while the other destroyer in a fixed position knocked out five enemy tanks. While operating in Noville, Double's biography noted, the unit was able to knock out a total of fourteen enemy tanks. One point of conflict; however, is the biography states this event took place on December 19, 1944—not the 20th, as Gerling had believed—but also highlights the fact that the units pulled out of the area of Noville on December 20, 1944. Attaining the rank of staff sergeant, Double later returned to Pennsylvania, married and became father to four children. The veteran spent forty-two years working at National Fuel, passed away on April 8, 2002 at the age of eighty-two and was laid to rest in Wintergreen George Cemetery in Erie, Pennsylvania.[59]

Pausing in reflection of the battle incident in which his friends were involved, Gerling said, "You know all those boys got for what they accomplished that day was a Bronze Star." He continued, "Years later, I think it might have been in the 1960s, Ricker went back on a tour of Europe and had the opportunity to visit several of the places he had served at during the war. They stopped in the town where they had knocked out all of those tanks and he found the very place where their Hellcat had been situated when fog had lifted all those years earlier."

Of further interest, Gerling explained, was that back in 1944, during the original tank encounter, a seven-year-old girl was living in one of the houses near the junction where the action unfolded. When Gerling's fellow 609th gunner, Ricker, returned to Luxembourg many years later, the same girl had grown into an adult and was still living in the house once owned by her mother, informing Ricker that she had been told that if "any of the American boys come through, take care of them with coffee and donuts." Gerling added, "But then she also said that her mother had said that those boys shouldn't have driven through her garden with their tanks," he laughed.

* * *

---

[59] TankDestroyer.net, *Justin Deryle Double*, www.tankdestroyer.net.

On the evening of December 24, 1944, Gerling was informed that he would finally be sent to join the fight that was raging in Bastogne. He and his tank commander, Sgt. Alan Iler, soon received orders transferring them to a new tank crew; however, their entry into the fray would wait a few hours when they received the opportunity to enjoy a Christmas meal hosted by a gracious family in Luxembourg City.

"The afternoon of Christmas eve, a family in Luxembourg invited me and Sergeant Iler over to their house for dinner," Gerling recalled.

There is scant information available on Allen Iler; however, limited records accessed through the Social Security Administration show that the Midway, Georgia, veteran was born on May 2, 1919 and passed away on April 3, 1995 at seventy-five years of age. Records located through the U.S. Archives indicate that his service began when he enlisted in the Georgia National Guard on September 16, 1940. Battalion records note that Sgt. Iler was later wounded on March 1, 1945 during operations in Trier, Germany.

On Christmas Eve 1944, prior to entering the Battle of the Bulge, Gerling was invited to enjoy dinner with a local Luxembourgish family. From left: Michael Stihl; Norbert Gerling; Alan Iler (sergeant in charge of Gerling's Hellcat); Stihl's daughter, Maxine; Stihl's wife (name unknown); and Paul (last name unknown, Stihl's son-in-law). *–courtesy of Norbert Gerling*

"The family we stayed with treated us great," Gerling said. "I can still remember the father's name—Michael Stihl, spelled just the same as the chainsaw company."[60]

The family's house, Gerling said, was a comfortable, thee-story structure with more than modest furnishings, leaving the young soldier

---

[60] Here Gerling is referring to Stihl, Inc., which was founded by Andreas Stihl in Stuttgart, Germany in 1926. Though the company has gained recognition for building quality yard equipment, chainsaws have become their best-known product throughout the years. See www.stihlusa.com.

with the impression that the family was fairly well off, although the meager meal they soon consumed would indicate otherwise under ordinary circumstances.

Gerling recalled, "All they had for dinner was potato soup made from the potato peels and then there was some kind of dessert. Folks over there were really having a hard time back then and food was often very hard to come by with the war going on. We ended up staying at their home until sometime around 2:00 a.m. Christmas morning, and that's when they came and picked us up to take us into the Bulge."

Loading up on an Army Jeep, Gerling still recalls the "eerie feeling" he and Sergeant Iler experienced during their trip toward the battered city of Bastogne, surrounded by the pungent smell of burnt sawdust and smoking craters along with the view of half-exploded trees and snow-covered timber littering the countryside. Drawing upon the experience he would acquire as a farmer in the years following the war, Gerling chose to describe the scene of the areas he passed during the Battle of the Bulge as terrain that "looked as though it had been run over by a huge brush hog."

Gerling's first destination in the battered Bastogne was in the small basement of a church, as underground rooms in the area had become premium real estate since they could provide the beleaguered soldiers with a little protection from a well-placed "screaming mimi"—the nickname given by American troops to German rockets such as the Nebelewerfer 41 because of the loud, howling noise made by the incoming projectiles. It also provided the troops with a little comfort from

The aid station for the 20th Armored Infantry Battalion, 10th Armored Division, located on Rue Neaufchateau in Bastogne, Belgium, was destroyed by German bombs on Christmas Eve, December 24, 1944. While waiting in the basement of a nearby church on Christmas morning, Gerling recalls hearing the thundering of the continued air strikes, which, hours earlier, leveled the aid station. *United States Army photograph*

the frigid weather assailing anyone unfortunate enough to be operating outdoors. Gerling and Sergeant Iler continued to wait in the church's basement until morning, with nothing more for breakfast other than a small block of cheese and some coffee.

"I can assure you that there wasn't much sleep anyone got that morning," he said, "because several hours earlier the Germans bombed the hospital nearby ... and you could hear all of that going on." Softly, he added, "We lost a lot of boys in that one and you just waited and wondered if one of those [German] bombs would get you next."

An article on the U.S. Army website describes the event Gerling mentions. On Christmas Eve 1944, when the skies cleared in the vicinity of Bastogne. This created the ideal conditions for the German Luftwaffe (Air Force) to send some of their bomber squadrons over the city. As the article goes on to explain, a "500-pound bomb fell directly on the 20th AIB [Armored Infantry Battalion] Aid Station, instantly killing 30 wounded U.S. soldiers in addition to Army nurse Renee Lemaire. On the following day, the remaining wounded were taken to the 101st headquarters at the Heintz Barracks where they remained until Gen. George S. Patton's 3rd Army arrived on Dec. 26.[61]

An M-36 Tank Destroyer is pictured crossing a snow-blanketed field in Dudelange, Luxembourg on January 3, 1945. Gerling noted that the M-18 Hellcats operated similar to a car when traversing icy surfaces, slipping and sliding because the steel tracks often found difficulty when trying to gain traction. –*United States Army Signal Corp photograph #ETO-HQ-45-5944 (Hustead)*

When first light broke over the horizon, he and Sergeant Iler were introduced to their new gun crew, as Gerling was slated to replace a gunner who had been medically evacuated because of a severe frostbite

---

[61] King, *African Nurse Saved GIs*, www.army.mil.

The Lucky Ones

injury to his foot.[62] For the next month, he would remain assigned to this "temporary" tank crew.

"It really wasn't very long before the Germans had become weakened to the extent that we just kept pushing them back [toward Germany]," Gerling said. "Most of the time, our operations involved moving in front of the infantry to remove any obstacles ... whatever it took to advance. It always seemed like I was one of the lucky ones—I always seemed to be at the right spot at the right time," he quipped.

The casualties incurred by American troops continued to mount as the Battle of Bastogne progressed, which frequently included soldiers of the 609th Tank Destroyer Battalion. For Gerling, whether it was divine providence or sheer luck, he was able to avoid serious injury, but some of the fellow soldiers with whom he served suffered circumstances during this period that would have grim and deadly effects years after the war.

A native of Waukesha, Wisconsin, Staff Sergeant Richard H. Beaster "distinguished himself in the siege of Bastogne, by knocking out seven German tanks while serving with the 609th Tank Destroyer Battalion ...." Newspaper accounts indicate that Beaster went missing on December 20, 1944 after "he was severely burned in rescuing fellow crewmen from [a] disabled tank ... [and] attempted to escape with a jeep behind the lines."[63] During this escape effort, the driver of the Jeep was killed by German troops and Beaster was taken prisoner. Months later, the tanker was freed from a prison camp by the Russians after Germany surrender. Sadly, on December 16, 1955, Beaster died of tuberculous he had contracted while imprisoned during the war.

---

[62] Frostbite and other cold weather injuries are issues that have plagued military forces for centuries. Between the autumn of 1944 and spring of 1945, the U.S. Army reported 46,000 cases of weather related injuries in the European Theatre. And although an estimated 10-percent of American casualties during World War II were found to be weather related, enemy forces also suffered greatly since German forces, between December 1941 and January 1942, suffered 100,000 cases of frostbite while operating in the Easter Theatre, with many of these cases requiring amputation. McCallum, *Military Medicine*, 85.

[63] December 17, 1955 edition of the *Waukesha Daily Freeman*.

Jeremy Paul Ämick

The thirty-four-year-old combat veteran was buried in Prairie Home Cemetery in his home community of Waukesha, Wisconsin.[64]

The platoons of the various companies within the 609th, including that of Company C of which Gerling was a member, frequently were employed in an artillery capacity in addition to being called upon to establish listening posts in operational sectors in and around Bastogne. Such activities placed the tank destroyers in harm's way and required quick defensive responses since they would encounter mortar and artillery fire when they approached enemy gun emplacements. The speed of the Hellcats also played a significant role in Company C's success when they were oftentimes sent into action to engage and destroy enemy tanks attempting to enter the outskirts of Bastogne and other American-held operational sectors.

"As the gunner, it was my decision on what type of ammunition I would use in a specific situation," Gerling said. "We only used two types while I was in Europe—the first was AP (armor piercing) and the other was HE (high explosive). If a target looked vulnerable, I would use the HE but if it looked like it needed more of a punch, I would use the AP," which, he further explained, possessed a soft outer casing similar to lead that would essentially stick to the side of an enemy tank and not glance off. As the round attached to the armor, this afforded its hard core the time necessary to burn through and essentially "ricochet everywhere inside the tank."

The enemy would not serve as the greatest aggravation during their time in combat. Gerling noted that the weather they were forced to endure helped deliver another slate of challenges for the GIs who were simply trying to survive during one Belgium's coldest winters in recorded history. In the book *Bastogne: The First Eight Days*, author SLA Marshall provides an account of ground so frozen that track vehicles no longer had to worry about becoming bogged in the mud, instead they were able to move over the hills in almost any direction. Marshall added: "Increasing cold, light winds and deep drifts changed many of the characteristics of the battle," which soon became a problem for

---

[64] Find A Grave Memorial, *Richard H. Beaster*, Findagrave.com.

commanders who were trying to find ways "to get their men indoors to keep them from freezing." The book also explained that the weather was frigid to the extent that many of the local Belgian villagers opted to remain in the comfort of their homes despite the German attacks unfolding around them, but were soon evacuated to provide shelter and protection for the infantry troops who came to occupy the area.[65]

Dean Chapman, a former officer in the 10th Armored Division to which Gerling's battalion was attached, explained that during the timeframe of November 20th through December 23rd 1944, the temperatures generally "ranged from the low teens to mid 20's." Chapman also stated that some occasions "it snowed heavily with driving winds and sleet, and at other times there were just flurries and fog" to help multiply the misery.[66]

"The cold—it was terrible ... terrible," Gerling grumbled. "I don't know how we ever survived it. You didn't take your boots off when you tried to sleep because you wouldn't be able to get them back on the next day because they would be frozen stiff. You eventually just reached a point where you could sleep in a snow bank because you got so tired and couldn't keep your eyes open any longer."

It was not only the soldiers who encountered problems with regard to the weather conditions. According to Gerling, some of their tank destroyers were occasionally limited in their movement in the region surrounded by snow-covered evergreens.

"The Hellcats were just like cars on the ice—they would slip and slide and it would create a dangerous situation, but you just took it easy and you could get around alright. The engines seemed to start easy enough, though, and I don't really remember having too many weather-related problems with them. Those radial engines were pretty doggone rugged and we had very few mechanical problems with them, at least as far as I remember."[67]

---

[65] Marshall, Bastogne: The First Eight Days, 106.

[66] Chapman, *Growl of the Tiger*, 53.

[67] The later M18 models, such as those that would have been used in the ETO by Gerling and the 609th, used a Continental R-975 C4 9-cylinder air cooled radial engine built by Buick. The motor had an output of 400 horsepower. Zaloga, M18 Hellcat Tank Destroyer, 12-13.

Jeremy Paul Ämick

Some battalions attempted to address the slippery conditions by welding ice cleats to the tracks of the tank destroyers, which then resulted in much greater problems since the heat generated during the bonding procedure often damaged the rubber track bushings. In the end, the primary means by which to address cold-weather mobility concerns was to provide the drivers with driving practice at every possible opportunity.

The platoons comprising Company C participated in several actions while supporting elements of the 502nd and 506th Airborne Regiments, repelling enemy incursions and filling any gaps in existing—yet frequently wavering—defenses. This created enough time for the 101st Airborne Division to organize their defenses for Bastogne and dissolve the German offensive measures. By the close of the Bastogne engagement in late January 1945, official records of Company C, 609th Tank Destroyer note that although three M-18s were lost, the company was able to destroy twenty-three German tanks, two 88mm guns and several vehicles. These successes, sadly, were tempered by the loss of seven soldiers killed in action, twenty-four wounded and two missing. The company effectively accomplished their mission of ensuring the vital road center of Bastogne was kept from the clutches of the battle-weary German Army.

"These units distinguished themselves in combat against powerful and aggressive enemy forces composed of elements of eight German divisions during the period from 18 to 27 December 1944 by extraordinary heroism and gallantry in defense of the key communications center of Bastogne, Belgium.... Without benefit of prepared defenses, facing almost overwhelming odds and with very limited and fast-dwindling supplies, these units maintained a high combat morale and an impenetrable defense, despite extremely heavy bombing, intense artillery fire, and constant attacks from infantry and armor on all sides of their completely cut-off and encircled position,"[68] wrote G.C. Marshall, in orders awarding

---

[68] Collins, *The Tigers of Bastogne*, 243-244.

The Lucky Ones

several elements of the 10th Armored Division a Distinguished Unit Citation[69] for their participation in a key battle of the war.[70]

The citation, which notes Company C, 609th Tank Destroyer Battalion less 1st Platoon, with 2nd Platoon Reconnaissance Company attached, essentially excluded Gerling from qualifying for the recognition since 1st Platoon (to which he belonged) was cut-off from the main element on the way to Luxembourg City when much of their equipment was damaged by enemy aircraft. However, Gerling explained, since he entered the Bulge as a replacement gunner on Christmas morning, which was within the timeframe covered by the citation, he was authorized to receive and wear the venerated recognition.

On January 20, 1945, a day that remains etched in the veteran's memory because it was the birthday of his then-fiancée Elizabeth, Gerling was reassigned to his original tank crew. Days later, the Battle of the Bulge came to a close with the Germans being pushed back to the positions they held prior to the offensive—a costly conflict resulting in 67,000 American and more than 100,000 German casualties.

The soldiers of the 609th then began to take account of the battering they had endured at the hands of enemy forces while making preparations for the next step of their overseas adventure, which would carry them deep into the German countryside to help deliver the *coup de grâce* to the enemy

---

[69] The Distinguished Unit Citation is now called the Presidential Unit Citation and was established through Executive Order No. 9075, dated 26 February 1942. The citation is "awarded to units of the Armed Forces of the United States and co-belligerent nations for extraordinary heroism in action against an armed enemy occurring on or after 7 December 1941. The unit must display such gallantry, determination, and *esprit de corps* in accomplishing its mission under extremely difficult and hazardous conditions as to set it apart and above other units participating in the same campaign." The Outpost Harry Survivors Association, *Distinguished Unit Citations*, http://www.ophsa.org/index.htm.

[70] See *Appendix B*.

Chapter 6

Germany and beyond ...

Public Domain

There were four of us [Hellcats] that went into the valley," he said. "We went through in a cluster because if we went through one at a time, we believed the German gun would then have the opportunity to take out each of our tanks one shot at a time ... just picking us off." – Gerling discussing his participation in the rescue of a stranded tank in early 1945.

The units who had spent the last several weeks fighting well-disciplined German forces in the deadly "Bulge" were soon rewarded a welcome reprieve. For a period of several days, they were given the

Jeremy Paul Ämick

time to replenish expended resources, process the replacements that would help restore their personnel strength close to previous levels and train for the upcoming push into the German mainland.

What came next were the detailed plans and preparations for the crossing of the Saar River, which involved clearing the fortifications along the riverfront with Company C, 609th to provide direct fire support for the operation. According to historical records, the company's efforts during this event resulted in the neutralization or destruction of more than forty enemy pillboxes, an achievement that essentially cleared the vicinity for the river crossing.[71]

Company C continued their movement in a westerly direction, supporting elements of the 10th Armored Division (shoulder patch pictured at the beginning of this chapter)—which included support of the 376th Infantry Regiment—and assaulting enemy positions that were oftentimes situated on higher ground. In the waning days of February 1945, the 10th Armored Division approached the vicinity of Trier, capturing the German town only days later on March 2, but not before incurring heavy casualties; hundreds of German soldiers were also killed and more than five hundred prisoners taken. Reports note that although German tanks were not a significant factor in the defense of the city, the offensive capabilities offered by the M-18 Hellcats of the 609th became an integral component to the success of the operation. The tank destroyers were able to destroy scores of German artillery pieces that had been raining their hellfire down upon the approaching American forces.

The intensity of their wartime undertakings had kept the troops of his battalion focused and busy, but when the city was eventually secured, Gerling recalls the capture of a German storage cellar during the brief break that followed. His fellow soldiers, he mirthfully explained, embraced stumbling upon the contents of the structure ... initially. However, the content soon delivered upon them a certain level of "discomfort," leaving them to wish they had let it be.

"We came upon a warehouse that was full of German champagne," he said. "It was three levels high with stacks on top of stacks

---

[71] *A Mini History,* Ahrenholz, 1.

of champagne bottles in holders on every level—it was more than you could have imagined! Everyone got all the champagne they wanted to drink but none of us really knew what in the world we were getting into," he grinned.

As the unsuspecting soldiers soon realize, the champagne that was stored on the upper levels and became among the first of the bottles to be liberated was of rather recent vintage, which, Gerling explained, left most of his fellow soldiers with distressed bowels following their mass consumption.

"One of the guys we were with said that he had dreamed of someday washing his feet in champagne," Gerling said. "That day, he removed his helmet, filled it with champagne and washed his feet right there at that warehouse," Gerling chuckled. "It was a dream come true for him!"

Over the course of the next couple of weeks, their push toward the Rhine included the capture of several smaller cities and the crossing of lesser rivers, occasionally requiring them to wait for the engineering companies supporting their movements to finish constructing the pontoon bridges they used in the crossings.

* * *

On March 7, 1945, Gering and his fellow crewmates aboard the M-18 Hellcat were unexpectedly afforded the opportunity to demonstrate their combat mettle on an applied scale when called upon to support a stranded American tank crew in dire need of assistance near the German city of Trier.[72]

"There was one of our tanks sitting right in the middle of this valley," explained Gerling, "and it had been disabled to the point that they couldn't fire their gun or anything—they were sitting ducks."

Although unscathed, the tank crew was trapped in the open after being struck by an 88mm German anti-tank gun that was mounted on a railcar, which, Gerling added, was partially concealed under an

---

[72] Trier is the oldest city in Germany and located along the Moselle River approximately six miles from the border of Luxembourg.

overpass on a hill overlooking the valley. The position of the German gun provided a vantage point that was ideal for picking off any approaching American armor. An article appearing on Warfare History Network explained that although the Germans originally designed the 88mm to serve in an anti-aircraft capacity, they were able "to learn and adapt as the war progressed, improving the antiaircraft fire capabilities of the weapon and they successfully modified it for tank, antitank, and related ground roles."[73]

"There were four of us [Hellcats] that were sent into the valley to assist the tank," he said. "We went through in a cluster because if we went through one at a time, we believed the German gun would then have the opportunity to take out each of our tanks using one shot at a time ... just picking us off."

When in a position where he could view the German artillery piece, Gerling noticed there were two pedestals that appeared to support the weight of the overpass. As the gunner, he used the tank's "ten-power scope" to sight in on the enemy threat.

"Once I had it sighted, I fired seven or eight rounds (from the tank's 76mm cannon), Gerling said. "I hit the two pedestals that I could see through the scope and the overpass collapsed onto the top of the German gun, neutralizing the threat."

Gerling noted that Lady Luck might have made an appearance that day since a German soldier who appeared to be untrained and lacked familiarity with the weapon's application in combat, operated the rail gun that fired upon him and his fellow tanks during their approach.

"By that time, it was close to the end of the war and [the Germans] were pulling older people and kids into service to help them fight ... people without any military experience," he said. "I'm pretty sure that the guy firing that rail gun had to be one of these people because he seemed to be such a bad shot, which turned out to be lucky for us."

With the deadly threat now removed, Gerling's Hellcat moved toward the stranded crew.

---

[73] Warfare History Network, *WW II Weapons: The German 88mm Gun*, https://warfarehistorynetwork.com.

The Lucky Ones

"A man came out of the tank and introduced himself as Captain Sanders and told us he was the tank commander," said Gerling. "I was hoping that I would be able to track him down and visit with him about what all happened on that day, but I was never able to actually locate him."[74]

For his participation in the rescue of the stranded tank, on July 5, 1945, Gerling was awarded a Bronze Star Medal for his "heroic achievement in connection with a military operation against an enemy of the United States at Trier, Germany," a copy of his orders read. Years later, as he reflected on his World War II experiences, Gerling affirmed that this remained one of the most memorable encounters of his time spent as a Hellcat gunner.

"Usually we were involved in skirmishes involving German tanks, but it was nice to be part of a team that helped rescue someone," Gerling said. "It was really a very important event to me because ...well," he paused, "you just don't know if what you did might have saved a person's life."

* * *

The battalion's resolute thrust into the German homeland continued to meet with pockets of resistance for the next several days, but American forces appeared to be on an unstoppable trajectory. Gerling and his fellow tankers were boosted by each individual soldier's desire to finish the war and return home to the states and the quiet lives they had left behind. As Gerling realized, however, the sordid fact remained even though the war possessed all appearances of approaching its end, the threat of harm facing everyone in the battalion was a prevalent concern.

---

[74] In a 10th Armored Division historical book, Gerling located a personnel listing that included the name of Captain Hubert Sanders of Florida, who was very likely the commander of the tank that was rescued on March 7, 1945. Research indicates that this listing refers to John Hubert Sanders who enlisted in the U.S. Army on November 1, 1942 at Camp Blanding, Florida. Born on April 26, 1918, Sanders passed away on May 31, 1999 and is buried in Ft. Myers Cemetery in Florida.

Jeremy Paul Amick

On the morning of March 12, 1945, tank destroyers from Company C's 2nd Platoon, accompanied by a light tank platoon from F Troop of the 43rd Cavalry Squadron, were departing the German community of Mertesdorf—a resort community in the Ruwer valley approximately five miles northeast from Trier. They were approaching the town of Kasel, to the southeast, where they were supposed to establish a roadblock. That is when tragedy struck in what became known at the Battle of the Rhine. One of the tanks from F Troop, which was leading the group, was immobilized when it detonated a land mine concealed in the roadway. German forces then began firing on the remaining tanks in the column with their anti-tank guns, resulting in the destruction or immobilization of four Hellcats, the loss of three Cavalry and resulted in the death of four Company C soldiers.

"Floyd Suber, from Florida, was the tank commander for one of those destroyers," said Gerling. "We always called him 'Happy' because he never seemed to be sad." Gerling continued," Our tank was about one hundred yards or so behind Suber's tank when they were hit—we had no idea there were so many Germans around and they just seemed to come out of nowhere. Things happened so fast that you were just concerned with the safety of your tank and defending your crew."

Gerling's Hellcat was far enough to the rear of the column that they were able to avoid the attention of German artillery and anti-tank guns. This fortuitous circumstance provided him and his comrades the opportunity to respond swiftly in evacuating those who had not been so fortunate.

"Suber was sort of blown out of his tank when they were hit." He added, "I don't know if it was the blast or the shrapnel, but it blew off part of his jaw and knocked one of his eyes out of the socket. We got him out of there and loaded him on the stretcher … and I remember him telling me that Hutchinson[75] had been killed. We never really knew

---

[75] Gerling refers to Corporal Clem Jervy Hutchinson, a fellow gunner in Company C, 609th TD who was killed in action on March 12, 1945. Hutchinson was a 1940 graduate of Tans Bay High School in Effingham, South Carolina, worked for Southern Bell Telephone after graduation and entered military service in September 1941. At the time of his death, Hutchinson's three brothers were all serving overseas. He is buried in Florence National Cemetery in Florence, South Carolina. The April 8, 1945 edition of the *Florence Morning News* (Florence, South Carolina).

what happened to [Suber]; we all thought that he had been killed, too, because of the seriousness of his injuries."

Sometime during the 1960s, Gerling explained, the 609th Tank Destroyer Battalion was having a reunion when their friend "Happy" unexpectedly sauntered into the room to join the festivities.

"Everyone thought we were looking at a ghost—we couldn't believe it!" said Gerling. "He later told me that what happened on the day that he had been injured."

Born December 4, 1920 in Greensboro, Florida, Floyd Elbert Suber Sr., lived his entire life in Florida, with the exception of the time he spent with the tank destroyers in World War II, during which he achieved the rank of sergeant first class. Following his wartime service, Suber married, raised three sons (one of whom preceded him in death) and a daughter. According to his obituary, he retired as a hardware salesman and passed away on August 6, 2008 at eighty-seven years of age. He is buried in Mt. Pleasant Cemetery in Chattahoochee, Florida with a marker denoting his military service and receipt of a Purple Heart medal.

The administration building of O'Reilly General Army Hospital in Springfield, Missouri, as it appeared during the height of its operation during World War II. During its five years of operation, the original 160-acre hospital site was home for 250 building including barracks, a Post Exchange, gymnasium and a chapel. In later years, the site became home to Evangel University. *Used by permission of the Betty A. Chase Evangel University Archives, O'Reilly Collection.*

Suber informed Gerling and his fellow former tank destroyers that following the near-deadly movement to Kasel, he was evacuated to a field hospital in Germany and was eventually transferred to O'Reilly General Hospital in Springfield, Missouri, where he was treated for his injuries. Part of his recovery,

Gerling said, required the reconstruction of Suber's jaw; however, he went on to enjoy a long and rich life in his native home of Florida.

O'Reilly General Army Hospital was established in 1941 and went on to serve more than 100,000 patients during the five years it was in operation, which included 42,000 wounded and injured soldiers, 60,000 military dependents and a number of prisoners of war. The hospital quickly gained a reputation for reconstructive and plastic surgery expertise during the World War II period. The facility closed as an Army hospital in September 1946 and later operated as a Department of Veterans Affairs hospital for more than five years. In late 1954, the property was purchased by the General Council of the Assemblies of God and was transformed into Evangel College. The site is now home to Evangel University and only one building remains from the O'Reilly General Army Hospital era.[76]

The late Emylou Keith, formerly of Jefferson City, was working as a nurse at O'Reilly Army Hospital in Springfield, Missouri, when she helped treat a soldier for a severe jaw injury. She believes it to have been Floyd Suber Sr., who was injured in 1944 while serving with Gerling in Germany.
– *Courtesy of Emylou Keith*

"[Suber] actually went through a long process that took quite a few operations," Gerling said. "They actually rebuilt his jaw using sheep bones, which is absolutely amazing. I don't know how the doctors were able to do something like that."

During a 2015 interview with Jefferson City, Missouri, resident Emylou Keith, she described her experiences of completing her training as a nurse at Wesley Hospital in Wichita, Kansas in 1944.[77] The same year, her

---

[76] Missouri Digital Heritage, *O'Reilly General Hospital*, http://cdm16795.contentdm.oclc.org/cdm/landingpage/collection/oreillyhosp.

[77] After the war, Keith was married and worked in several nursing and administrative positions, eventually moving to Jefferson City to work for the Missouri State Board of Nursing. She passed away in Jefferson City on February 25, 2017 and was laid to rest in White Chapel Memorial Gardens in Wichita, Kansas.

brother, Bud Gaffney, who was serving as a pilot with the U.S. Army Air Forces, lost his life when he was shot down over Japan. Seeking to honor the memory of their brother and filled with the patriotic fervor of a nation at war, she and her sister then made application for commission as nurses in the Army Nurse Corps and went on to attend basic training at Camp Carson, Colorado. The newly trained nurses were then extended the opportunity to select from a number of stateside assignments before being shipped overseas to treat wounded servicemembers. For Keith and her sister, the choice was simple.

"We asked for Springfield (Missouri) because I thought we'd at least be able to get home to see my parents before going overseas," Keith said.

The sisters' request was granted and they continued their training at the O'Reilly Army Hospital in Springfield. The Army, Keith explained, later discovered she had a perforated eardrum and believed exposure to loud noises in a combat environment might lead to irreparable damage. The sisters were separated a few months later when Keith remained at the hospital and her sister was transferred to serve as a nurse in India. While stationed at the Army hospital in Springfield, Keith was eventually placed as a nurse in charge of one of the wards overseeing "ambulatory patients, all of whom were able to get up and around, except for two of them."

Floating bridges, such as the one pictured above, were constructed by engineer outfits across Germany to help support various river crossings. The bridge, which was erected by the 85th Engineers in Worms, Germany, supported the crossing of 3,040 vehicles in its first twenty-four hours of operation. *United States Army photograph*

Keith added, "One of the patients was severely burned and confined to a bed, and the other one had his lower jaw shot (or blown) off in combat."

Jeremy Paul Ämick

In discussing the patient with the jaw injury, Keith explained that corrective surgeries were performed to reconstruct his jaw using the bones from sheep. Although the passage of decades and the sheer number of patients she helped treat have removed any memory of this particular patient's name, given the timing and nature of his injury, she believes it was likely Gerling's friend and fellow tank destroyer, Floyd Suber.

Following the evacuation of Suber and others who were injured in combat near Kael, the 609th Tank Destroyer Battalion progressed into the heart of Germany. During the waning days of March 1945, Company C, which was still assigned to the 10th Armored Division and ultimately under the command and control of the Third Army, arrived in the vicinity of Queichheim, southwest of Mannheim and Heidelberg. The division was then moved from under the Third Army and placed under the command and control of the Seventh Army. It was during this period that the battalion received the welcome respite of a few days of down time while they waited for the 85th Engineers to erect a bridge across the Rhine east of Worms, Germany.

* * *

This photograph shows an M-18 from the CCB section of the 609th as it waits to cross the bridge constructed across the Neckar River in Mannheim, Germany on March 30, 1945. – *Courtesy of NARA*

While waiting for the engineers to complete their work on the floating bridge, Gerling and his crew decided to "kill a little time" until their next movement orders arrived. Walking through brush near the river, the young soldier was startled when a pheasant erupted from the overgrowth and flew in front of him. A little while later, after hearing Gerling recount the incident, a few of his fellow destroyers decided a brief hunting expedition might provide them a welcome break from their frenetic cross-country travels.

The Lucky Ones

"Me and some of the other guys [in Company C] decided to go look for the pheasant and ended up scaring it up again," Gerling said. "Just like the first time, it flew right in front of me and I [instinctively] raised up my carbine and shot it." With a wide grin, he affirmed, "That's the only pheasant I ever shot and I still tell everyone that I have a one hundred percent record when it comes to shooting pheasants."

* * *

According to an official history compiled by the 85th Engineers, their participation in "The Rhineland Operation" began in earnest on the afternoon of March 25, 1945 when they established a command post in a house fifty feet from the approach to the bridge site at the city of Worms, Germany. The next day, Allied artillery fired barrages across the Rhine River and assault forces crossed in several waves to secure the far shore and establish a bridgehead. Construction of a Class 40 Pontoon Bridge began at 6:00 a.m. on March 26 and was open to traffic by 3:12 p.m. that afternoon. Once completed, the bridge spanned an impressive 1,047 feet from abutment to abutment and "consisted of 131 pontoons, and two trestles on both the far and near shore." During its first twenty-four hours in operation, 3,040 vehicles used the bridge for crossing.[78]

On March 28, the 609th made the crossing, which, Gerling explained, "really led us into the mainland of Germany."

The crossing of the Rhine occurred in several locations, but the initial crossing that set the stage for subsequent crossings was known as *Operation Varsity*—the largest airborne assault of all time. This operation began on the morning of March 24, 1945 and involved nearly 17,000 paratroopers and thousands of Allied aircraft from two Allied divisions—the British Sixth Airborne Division and the U.S. 17th Airborne Division. Though there were problems that occurred as the operation unfolded, it was considered a success since Allied forces were able to secure a foothold in western Germany, capturing bridges

---

[78] The 85th in Germany, *The Rhineland Operation*, www.85th-engineer.com

and securing towns that would be used for the Allied advance in the coming days.[79]

There were certainly a number of wartime incidents that were imprinted in Gerling's reflections, one of which occurred during their westward push. As the veteran explained, a frequent scene they began to witness was the scores of "displaced people around that time who had no home ... they were just walking around the countryside looking for something to eat and a place to sleep."

Throughout this period, the battalion was often split up by platoons and attached to different combat commands under the 10th Division—1st platoon of Company C of the 609th Tank Destroyer Battalion was attached to the 634th Field Artillery Battalion. The group was then given the assignment to provide local security and neutralize threats such as 88mm guns and anti-tank weapons encountered along the way.

The battalion soon arrived in Heidelberg where, Gerling said, "we discovered this huge depot that was full of musical instruments. Everyone (in the battalion) grabbed whatever instrument could be found and played it the best they could. I found a guitar and just plucked away at it for a little while," he smiled. "From then on," he continued, "you just kind of went from day to day, never really knowing what would happen next but we kind of knew things were coming to a close."

The company's southeasterly push carried them to the vicinity of Crailsheim, Germany by the second week of April 1945, where they encountered a significant—and unexpected—level of resistance by an enemy they all prayed would soon lose any remnants of a will to fight. The *Wehrmacht* may have suffered immense losses at the hands of the Allies but the German forces were still able to hammer the American forces at "Crailsheim with concussion bombs and shells, burned it with incendiaries, assaulted it with whole battalions of infantry."[80] (The Wehrmacht was the unified military of Germany from 1935-1946 and consisted

---

[79] Wright, *The Last Drop*, Introduction.

[80] *Terrify and Destroy: The Story of the 10th Armored Division*, a small booklet covering the history of the 10th Armored Division. This booklet is one of the series of G.I. Stories published by the Stars & Stripes in Paris in 1944-1945. Accessed through www.lonesentry.com.

of the *Heer* (Army), the *Kriegsmarine* (Navy) and the *Luftwaffe* (Air Force)). The destruction that would occur in the town of Crailsheim was not a new occurrence, as its "first tale of destruction begins in 1379 when the city was under attack by not one, but three different imperial cities." During World War II, Crailsheim would experience the shock of near destruction, as only "one building survived the heavy bombardment, the *Johanneskirche*, or Saint John's Church." Yet the town has thrived in the decades following the end of the war and continues to host the Frankish Folk Festival every September, which boasts 200,000 guests annually who visit for the food, entertainment and fun ... and possibly to visit the stalwart Saint John's Church.[81]

During the combat that unfolded in and around Crailsheim in World War II, it was bestowed the moniker of "Second Bastogne" by many of the soldiers who participated in the conflict and witnessed the significant number of casualties incurred. The battle here also become an event Gerling would have to witness from the sidelines because of an injury he sustained only days previous.

"That [Crailsheim] was one of the areas where I was extremely lucky," prefaced Gerling. "A week or ten days before we went into the area, we were stopped and I began putting up a little tent after we had stopped for a rest. I was driving the stakes into the ground using an axe [with one side of the head of axe similar to a hammer]." He continued, "While I was pounding one of the stakes into the ground, a guy walked behind me dragging some kind of rope that caught the end of the axe, and I ended up hitting my knee with the end of the axe and splitting it open pretty bad."

Fortunately, his kneecap was not shattered but the injury was critical enough that he was no longer capable of bending his leg, which meant he was unable to negotiate his way into or out of the Hellcat.

"They wanted to send me to the hospital but I wouldn't go ... because I knew I would probably never get back to my boys."

For the next two weeks, the injured gunner was placed in Headquarters Company, following the movements of Company C as a

---

[81] My German City, *Crailsheim*, www.mygermancity.com.

passenger in supply trucks or with the kitchen crew, until his knee healed to the extent he could crawl back into his Hellcat.

While Gerling was recuperating from his injury and as the 609th Tank Destroyer Battalion continued to press the Germans toward surrender, he was temporarily replaced as a gunner by Sergeant Joseph Mosetti, a fellow Company C soldier from Baltimore, Maryland. Gerling described Mosetti "as a floater who filled in wherever he was needed," and who had also taken Gerling's place when he transferred to a different platoon during the Battle of the Bulge only weeks earlier.[82]

Gerling reiterated that he and his fellow soldiers realized the war they were fighting could not be very far from its end, as evidenced by an increase in the desperation of the German forces. This was a situation, he recalls, growing more obvious since their enemies were required to make do with dwindling levels of equipment and supplies—and Crailsheim is where their enemy really began to exhibit the hopelessness of their cause.

The unofficial history of the 609th Tank Destroyer Battalion goes on to describe that during the five days in Crailsheim, 1st platoon continued to provide local security for the 634th Field Artillery Battalion while engaged in other supporting operational roles. They were often placed in positions forward of the main element since their long-range firing capabilities were ideal for engaging the occasional anti-tank gun and

While racing between German towns during WWII, Gerling took a moment to snap this photograph of his M-18 as it sat in front of a building "somewhere across Germany." – *courtesy of Norbert Gerling*

---

[82] Born October 30, 1915, records accessed through Archives.com indicate that Joseph J. Mosetti died on July 7, 1997 while living in Baltimore City, Maryland, and was laid to rest in Oak Lawn Cemetery. Enlistment records accessed through www.archives.gov note that he entered the military on September 3, 1941 at Baltimore, Maryland, and that his occupation at the time was listed as the mechanical treatment of metals, such as forging.

The Lucky Ones

in removing obstacles encountered during their missions. The history confirms that although the German forces did not have many tanks at their disposable at this late point in the war, they made up for it with their significant number of 75-millimeter and 88-millimeter anti-tank weapons.

"In Crailsheim, we saw a lot of German towed artillery [rather than tanks], which was not very maneuverable," he said, but when combined with other resources, could still prove to be quite deadly for us," he added.

In the book *The Last Offensive*, a sordid picture is painted regarding the resistance encountered when reaching Crailsheim, although it describes the opening days of the operation in early April 1945 as "no more than that normally encountered in a breakthrough operation—demolished bridges, occasional roadblocks, small arms fire, antitank rockets." However, by April 7th, the American forces began to receive a battering from "stubborn clumps of German infantry supported by antitank guns,"—a hellish episode in their already lengthy combat travels accentuated by their armored columns being strafed by German planes.[83]

A study prepared by the Armored School at Fort Knox, Kentucky, between 1949 and 1950 reviewed the 10th Armored Division's actions during the Crailsheim Operation. The study highlighted several lessons learned that may have improved upon the division's successes. The study investigated such issues as maneuverability concerns that were attributable to the seasonal rains that "created quagmires of country side." An additional focus of the study were the instructions issued by higher headquarters that "were not always clear or specific" and thus created "doubt and confusion as to exactly what was desired of their units."[84]

There did exist an element of surprise at Crailsheim resulting in the outcome of some early successes by the American forces. Regardless, the 10th Division was ordered out of the area because Sixth Corps

---

[83] MacDonald, *The Last Offensive*, 417.

[84] The Armored School, *10th Armored in the Crailsheim Operation*, 79-80.

79

believed that the surprise attacks "could not be followed up due to our lack of infantry and intense enemy air and ground action." Shortly thereafter, the 609th Tank Destroyer Battalion and the remainder of the division left the area on April 11, 1945 without having secured a conclusive advantage. The five days of the operation in Crailsheim (April 5-10, 1945) resulted in American ground forces killing an estimated one thousand German soldiers and processing more than two thousand as prisoners of war.

The frenetic pace of their movement across either France or Germany never seemed to provide the soldiers of 609th with much time to grow bored or complacent with their surroundings, especially when they received the unexpected opportunity to witness new military developments such as one of the German Air Force's new fighter jets—the ME 262. Viewed by many historians as one of the most revolutionary aircraft of the Second World War, the Messerschmitt Me-262 acquired the distinction of becoming the first jet fighter to enter operational service with the air force of Germany. In the book *The Me 262 Stormbird*, authors Colin Heaton and Anne-Marie Lewis note that although the German pilots were the first to fly jet fighters in combat, they were also "plagued with a very tenuous and unpredictable array of technical problems, political intrigue, a growing shortage of fuel and munitions, losses of pilots and other critical assets, a growing, technologically proficient and dedicated enemy, and, perhaps most importantly, the fact that nearly every pilot that climbed into the cockpit of his jet knew that he was fighting a losing war." [85]

"One morning, around breakfast time, I remember seeing what they said were some of the first jet fighters developed by Germany," recalled Gerling. "They came barreling overhead and dropped a bomb, but it wasn't very accurate and completely missed whatever its target was. We all kind of sat around and laughed about it." With a grin, he added, "Fortunately, [the Germans] didn't get enough time in the war to really perfect those things."

---

[85] Heaton & Lewis, *The Me 262*, 1.

The dispiriting experience of an unfinished mission at Crailsheim now behind them, the next few weeks essentially became a race to the Alps, with the forces of the 10th Armored Division encountering diminishing levels of resistance. Gerling soon recovered from his knee injury and was able to return to his Hellcat crew during the final push. Passing through several small towns and villages along the way, such as Ohringen and Ulm, the 10th Division became a motivated and unstoppable German military-crushing machine. Throughout a number of these final drives, Gerling and 1st platoon continued to function as a security force with the 634th Field Artillery Battalion, continuing the 609th's previous practice of participating in marches, not as a battalion-level element, but rather as individual companies attached to various combat commands within the 10th Armored Division.

We passed by so many small cities so quickly, you just couldn't remember the names of all of them," said Gerling. "No one really took the time to stop and write it all down."

Toward the latter part of the war, Gerling shared, the soldiers of Company C received the opportunity to participate in an event he describes as "psychological warfare," using a touch of guile and deception to seize control of a German town without encountering any direct confrontation.

"The whole thing really didn't amount to much," said the veteran. "There was a small village that sat below a big bluff ... with a small stream between us and the village." He continued, "Someone got on a big bullhorn and told the people of the town to surrender—and they did after a little while," he affirmed. "Then, somebody went down there and took all of the German soldiers as prisoners of war."

Gerling also recalled that during the process of coaxing the townspeople into surrender, a couple of the German soldiers who had occupied the town decided they would "pull an easy one and get out of there before the Americans seized control." Gerling added. "The [German soldiers] began to walk off in the opposite direction, very nonchalantly as if no one would notice them." He further explained, "One of the gunners [in Company C] loaded up a round of high explosive and shot it between them—ended up taking them both out."

Jeremy Paul Ämick

The former soldier also noted that everyone in the battalion discovered that there were still many threats that existed even as the war appeared to be nearing an end, including those not directly related to the scorching fires of combat.

"There was a guy in our reconnaissance company who was good at neutralizing land mines," said Gerling, when discussing the service of Technical Sergeant Nicholas Seech.[86] "One time, he had one of these mines on the hood of his Jeep and was working on disarming it and somehow it went off," he added. "The guy was actually pretty lucky because the blast lifted him up and threw him back some distance, but he lived through it. I remember that he had a bunch of facial injuries—his face looked like sausage meat."

The battalion's unofficial history notes that Seech's injury occurred on May 1, 1945, while they were operating in the vicinity Garmisch-Partenkirchen. In later, years, Gerling recalls visiting with the wounded veteran during battalion reunions, marveling at his recovery from his injuries. He remarked, "Other than some small scars, you really couldn't even tell that something had even happened to him."

The 10th Armored Division and its supporting elements pursued their southerly thrust and, by the end April, arrived near the base of the Alps. It is here they assembled in the area that would serve as their rather comfortable home for the next several weeks and await the instructions that would eventually send them back to the states.

---

[86] Born on January 7, 1919, enlistment records accessed through the World War 2 U.S. Army Enlistment Archive notes that Nicholas Seech, a native of Pennsylvania, enlisted in the U.S. Army on October 20, 1941. According to his obituary in the August 2, 2001 edition of the *Pittsburgh Post-Gazette*, Seech passed away on August 1, 2001 in Munhall, Pennsylvania; was married and had three sons; and was employed at US Steel Homestead Works. See www.www2enlistment.org.

Chapter 7

Ready for home

Zugspitze, Public Domain

They were going to ship our tanks to Japan for the invasion of the Japanese mainland, but [President] Truman dropped the bomb and the Japanese surrendered. Luckily, we didn't have to go." – Gerling describing the weeks after the war ended in Germany.

Upon Germany's surrender on May 8, 1945, the soldiers of the 609th Tank Destroyer Battalion were traveling in a convoy near Garmisch-Partenkirchen, Germany, when they stopped for what would become a two-week break in action.[87]

---

[87] Situated at the base of the Bavarian Alps and an eighty-minute train ride from the city of Munich, Garmisch and Partenkirchen were "forcibly grafted together in 1935, under Hitler's orders, to host the next year's Winter Olympics." Russ Juskalian, *Alpine Interlude 80 Minutes From Munich*, appearing in the February 24, 2012 edition of *The New York Times*.

"Someone came around and told us all that the Germany had surrendered," Gerling said, "and I think it was sometime around 4 [o'clock] in the evening. Everybody started to celebrate ... a lot of the boys began shooting their guns in the air and cheering."

Gerling added that although he does not recall their celebration of victory in Europe being tinged with heavy imbibing, if anyone did choose to partake of alcohol, "it was what they had been able to gather somewhere along the way."

The veteran also noted that the local German community sponsored a celebration for the battalion that evening, bringing in music and hosting a dance for the soldiers. Smiling, Gerling said that during the celebration he "drank a little German beer ... and it was pretty stout!" He added, "The German people were sick of war and were as happy as we were that it had finally come to and end."

Although they were stationed in the same vicinity, the companies within the 609th Tank Destroyer Battalion made their temporary German homes in differently locations, with Company C setting up their area of operations in the small hamlet of Walchensee beginning in mid-May 1945.

A small tourism community located south of Munich, Walchensee sits along the pristine and beautiful Lake Walchen, thus providing a much-needed respite from the devastation, depredations and overall depressing environments that company had dealt with since landing in Europe nearly a year earlier.

"They told us that the lake," Gerling explained, "was about two miles wide, five miles long. It was also as clear as crystal. While there," he continued, the men of the company were able to "confiscate a boat

Gerling took this photograph of his assistant driver, Charlie Kuktis, in May 1945 as he stood near the summit of the ski slope in Garmisch-Partenkirchen that was used during the 1936 Olympics, an event, that to this day, was the biggest sporting event in the area's history. —courtesy of Norbert Gerling

or two" for purposes of fishing whenever they found some down time. "There were cabins around the lake and we all stayed in a building similar to a motel," he said. "The evenings could be pretty chilly but the area was very beautiful."

On one of their fishing outings, Gerling and a fellow company C soldier who, he affirmed, made the claim that he had a little fishing experience but was familiar with demolitions, took a small boat out on the lake a short distance. Once in what appeared to be a deeper area of the lake, they then submerged "a block of TNT" in an attempt to catch a mess of fish to fry up for a meal later.

"We used a long fuse and sunk it down to the bottom of the lake thinking we'd come up with a bunch of fish," he grinned, "but all we ended up with was a bunch of churned water and only a couple of fish. The second time around," he went on to explain, "we decided to use a much shorter fuse and I think I just about broke my oar trying to paddle away from that thing. But that time, we ended up with an entire mess of fish."

He added, "There was no combat when we got to the Alps but we did patrol the area to clean out any Germans that were trying to hide in the area," said Gerling, describing the days following the German surrender. "For pretty much the remainder of our time there, we began to receive the newer M-36 tanks—the old M-18s were just junked out by that time, I guess," he said. "Those 36s weren't that much better; they went from a 76-millimeter gun to a 90-millimeter, but they were really the same, so it wasn't that difficult to make the transition even though we never ended up using them in combat."

While serving as soldiers of the occupational forces of Germany, Gerling and his fellow Company C members had the opportunity for some sightseeing, including this picture he took of friends visiting an artesian well on Mt. Zugspitze—Germany's highest peak. *–courtesy of Norbert Gerling*

Jeremy Paul Ämick

He further noted, "To bide the time, we did nothing but maintenance on the tanks and then began transporting them to Nuremburg to prepare for shipment for the war in the Pacific," he said. "They were going to ship our tanks to Japan for the invasion of the Japanese mainland, but [President] Truman dropped the bomb and the Japanese surrendered. Luckily, we didn't have to go."

As part of a propaganda campaign to increase the birthrate among the German populace, Adolph Hitler instituted a three-tier medal called the *The Cross of Honor for the German Mother*, other times referred to as the *Mother's Cross*. The crosses were awarded based upon the number of children to which a mother gave birth—bronze, for a mother with four to five children; silver, for a mother with six to seven children, and gold, for eight or more children. –*courtesy of Norbert Gerling*

While on a break between tank drop-offs in Germany, Gerling recalled "nosing around" through a bombed-out industrial building, at which point he stumbled upon an interesting discovery.

The Lucky Ones

"I found a German Cross lying on the ground inside this building and picked it up and brought it home with me," he said. "We [soldiers] were always finding trinkets and things and would trade stuff with each other to bring back with us," he added.

The *Mother's Cross* was instituted in 1938 by Adolf Hitler, and was awarded as encouragement for German women to have more children. The type of medal varied according to the number of children a mother had. The cross Gerling discovered was bronze; therefore, it had been presented to a mother with four or five children.[88]

More than seventy years after retrieving the German decoration from the wreckage in Nuremburg, Gerling chose to share the history behind his discovery of the now-historic piece, donating it to the Cole County Historical Society in Jefferson City in January 2015 for display and educational purposes.

The time the battalion spent in Bavaria also introduced many of the men of Company C to a prisoner that later acquired the status of legend in the annals of the National Aeronautics and Space Administration (NASA) and Cold War history—the famed German rocket scientist, Wernher Von Braun. Prior to the war's end, the German scientist had worked in the country's rocket program at the Peenemünde site on the northeastern coast of Germany, receiving notoriety for assisting in the design and development of the deadly V-2 rocket. As the war progressed and it became obvious that Germany would have to surrender, Von Braun and members of his team moved to southern Germany so they would not have to surrender to the Russians and thus avoiding any barbarism for which they were reputed to employ when dealing with German prisoners.

Von Braun and his team of German scientists were captured by the 12th Armored Division at their installation in Kochel, north of the 609th Tank Destroyer Battalion's' accommodations on Lake Walchensee. The entire German facility, including Von Braun and his scientists, were moved to the United States as part of *Operation Paperclip*, becoming

---

[88] German History Documents, *The Cross of Honor for the German Mother*, http://germanhistorydocs.ghi-dc.org/.

part of a new experimental test station located at White Oaks, Maryland.[89] *Operation Paperclip* was the "codename under which the US intelligence and military services extricated scientists from Germany, during and after the final stages of World War II. The project was originally called *Operation Overcast*, and is sometimes also known as *Project Paperclip*." The operation resulted in more than 1,500 German scientists being brought to the United States in order to prevent the Soviet Union from acquiring Germany's scientific knowledge and, which in turn, led to the U.S. development of NASA and ICBM program.[90]

Prior to their departure from their homeland, Von Braun and his scientists became very renowned German prisoners of war through conversations between the soldiers of the 609th Tank Destroyer Battalion. Gerling would go on to participate in the provision of security for the installation used to house Von Braun and his fellow soldiers prior to their being moved to the United States.

"We all guarded the area where Von Braun and his team were being housed," recounted Gerling. "Our guard duty consisted of walking around the area—that's about all it amounted to," he added. "He wasn't about to leave, though, because he thought that the Germans would surely shoot him [because of the atrocities committed using the technologies he developed]." Gerling continued. "One of the guys from our company had the opportunity to visit with Von Braun and later told me that he was one of the smartest men he had ever spoken with."

In the years after the war, Von Braun was employed by NASA, serving as the director of the newly formed George C. Marshall Space Flight Center, later leading the development of the Saturn V booster. In July 1972, Von Braun resigned from NASA, becoming the "vice president for engineering and development with Fairchild Industries of Germantown, Maryland," and, three years later, helped establish the National Space Institute. The famed rocket scientist passed away from kidney cancer in 1977 at a hospital in Alexandria, Virginia, at sixty-five years of age.[91]

---

[89] Field, *The Capture of Werner Von Braun*, www.12tharmoredmuseum.com.

[90] Operation Paperclip, *Welcome to Operation Paperclip*, http://www.operationpaperclip.info/.

[91] Encyclopedia, *Wernher Von Braun Biography*, www.notablebiographies.com.

The Lucky Ones

* * *

In the early weeks of the post-war period, Gerling recalls many of the soldiers relaxing by engaging in some friendly games of softball just "to kill the time," which occasionally brought him into contact with some true sports professionals in addition to a handful of other intriguing individuals also serving in uniform.

"We would spend some of our free time playing softball in those early days," he said. "One of the guys that played on our softball team was named Victor DiSanza—and he was a great softball pitcher!" Gerling affirmed. "Vic was a left-hander and he'd release the ball real low and it would just climb on you. On top of that, he could pitch a game every day and never seemed to get a sore arm. He was friends with [St. Louis Cardinals Hall of Famer] Stan Musial; they had gone to high school together back in Pennsylvania. [DiSanza] was a great softball player and later was in [Stan] Musial's wedding."

Born January 5, 1919, Victor A. DiSanza was raised in the community Donora, Pennsylvania, passing away on October 16, 1992 at seventy-three years of age. The September 26, 1945 edition of *The Daily Republican* notes that Corporal DiSanza was discharged from the U.S. Army on September 25, 1945, a month prior to Gerling's release from service. Stan Musial was also born on November 21, 1920 and was also raised in Donora. He went on to play baseball for the St. Louis Cardinals from 1941-1963 and was inducted into the Baseball Hall of Fame in 1969. On January 19, 2013, Musial passed away in St. Louis, Missouri while under hospice care for Alzheimer's and was interred in Forever Bellerive Cemetery in Creve Coeur, Missouri.[92]

The June 30, 1945 edition of *The Tigers' Tale*—a newspaper published by the Tenth Armored Division while stationed in Garmisch-Partenkirchen—notes that the team for which Gerling played, alongside Vic DiSanza and other soldiers of the battalion, was runner-up for the Tenth Armored Division softball championship. They lost to the team comprised of members of the 423rd Armored Field Artillery Battalion, who secured the softball championship for the second year in a row.

---

[92] Baseball-Reference, *Stan Musial*, www.baseball-reference.com.

Jeremy Paul Amick

In the ensuing weeks, they remained part of the occupational forces of Germany and were not always engaged in routine and monotonous duties intended to keep the American soldiers occupied. They soon received word of an opportunity to "try out" for an event that would allow them to expand upon the baseball games they had been playing against other military teams by helping to introduce the beloved American past time to the German people.

Pictured above are members of the softball team comprised of members of Company C, 609th Tank Destroyer Battalion. Gerling (middle row, third person from left) played with Vic DiSanza (first row, first person), who was a classmate and close friend of St. Louis Cardinal great Stan Musial –*courtesy of Norbert Gerling*

"Like it did with many European nations, American servicemen brought the game of baseball to Germany during World War II. Germany, in particular, embraced the game and became one of the leaders in organizing an official European baseball league," notes the book *The Politics of Baseball*. [93]

---

[93] Briley, The Politics of Baseball, 145.

The Lucky Ones

With Germany divided into four occupational sectors that were controlled by either France, the Soviet Union, the United Kingdom and the United States, the American zone in the south embarked upon a coordinated effort "as part of the reconstruction process" to use baseball as a means to expose German youths to the "American Way of Life."[94]

"[The Army] sent out leaflets to different military units [in southern Germany] asking for people who wanted to try out for a baseball team," Gerling said. Once at the tryouts, Gerling noted that you had to essentially "fight your way onto the team" because of the number of soldiers who showed up to vie for a position.

"In sports you always wanted to prove that you were better than your opponent," Gerling said, describing the large number of those interested in introducing the American sport to the German populace. "Also," he continued, "we really had nothing to do at that time so this would allow us to keep busy doing something that we enjoyed."

Ninety-six aspiring players showed up to the practice, he recalled, a group that was soon whittled down to twenty-two potential players.

"The first thing they did was give you a bat and you had to be able to hit the ball. They ran me through the batting cage four different days so that I could prove myself as a hitter good enough to play on this type of team," Gerling said. "Luckily," Gerling mirthfully added, "they must have caught me in the better part of my career because I sailed right through the tryouts."

Initially placed in the second base position, the veteran explained that for some reason the team leadership did not like the manner in which he played the position. The decision was later made to move him to the right field position, which he continued to play the remainder of the time he spent with the team.

"They gave us some time to get oriented—to play together as a group ... something like spring training," he said. "When we started playing other teams, we probably didn't have to travel any farther than thirty or forty miles from Garmisch, but we would play two or three games a week against small leagues in different areas," he said. "There

---

[94] Baseball Reference, *History of Baseball in Germany*, www.baseball-reference.com.

Jeremy Paul Ämick

were times that we did get to play in some large stadiums, like one in Stuttgart that seated 85,000 people. You felt like you were playing in a rain barrel because there were hardly any spectators there."

The weeks passed by quickly as the young soldier continued to help transport the company's tank destroyers to Nuremberg on the days he was not playing baseball. As the end of summer of 1945 approached, the 609th received word that their days in Germany were now numbered since they were on a schedule to rotate back to the United States.

As the weeks progressed to the latter weeks of summer, Gerling and his fellow soldiers of the battalion traveled an assembly area command redeployment site at Camp Atlanta in Chalons, France, for the final preparation for their return to United States. They would board trains for the port in Rheims, France and departed Europe on August 30, 1945.[95] As indicated on Gerling's discharge papers, they arrived in New York Harbor eight days later.

"The boat they sent us home on was a small one, we called it a tub and just about everybody got sick," he grinned. "But it sure was fast. I also remember there was one guy in our outfit who really couldn't wait to get home," Gerling continued. "He said that he wanted to be the first one on the dock and when we pulled up into New York Harbor, he jumped into the water and swam ashore." This humorous event, Gerling asserted, heralded the beginning of the end of the relationship that he and his fellow tank destroyers had developed through nearly four years of service together. It was now time to focus on returning to his rural Missouri home and solidify the commitment he had made to Elizabeth Kempker several years earlier.

---

[95] The trains that the battalion road were boxcars called a Forty and Eight. The name is derived from "40/8" cargo capacity sign emblazoned on each French boxcar that had carried American doughboys to the front during the First World War and were later used in WWII. The term Forty and Eight meant that each boxcar had the capacity to hold either forty men or eight horses.

Chapter 8

A return to the quiet life

"Sergeant Gerling represents millions of members of the Greatest Generation, men and women who demonstrated the grit, courage and unshakeable optimism that made our country what it is today." – Former Missouri Governor Jay Nixon during a ceremony on January 21, 2015 in which Gerling was presented the French Legion of Honor in the Missouri Capitol.

"After we got off the ship, we all walked up a hill to a giant mess hall. We had been told that we could order anything that we wanted, so the first thing I ordered were two fried eggs." Pausing, with a grin, Gerling added, "I asked for two fried eggs because I hadn't had any in a year or so. I still love eggs. Another guy in our company, I remember, hollowed out a half-section of cantaloupe and then filled it full of ice cream! We were all just really happy to finally be back in the United States and have some of the food we'd been missing."

The combat veteran remained only a single night in New York and boarded a train bound for St. Louis the next day. He traveled to Jefferson Barracks in southern St. Louis, where he completed some additional paperwork to get a ticket, this time to board a train bound for Jefferson City. Upon his arrival, he placed a telephone call to his sister who then came to pick him up from the train station downtown.

"I was able to stay home for thirty days or so and then I had to report back to Jefferson Barracks to process out of the Army," he said, noting that he received his "official" separation from the military on October 21, 1945.

The combat veteran did not engage in passing idle time as he soon followed in the footsteps of his grandfather and father by embarking upon his lifelong career.

"In early 1946 I started farming and have never retired," he smiled. "I was out working in the fields yesterday," he confidently added during a 2014 interview.

Norbert and Elizabeth Gerling in their wedding photograph from February 23, 1946.
–courtesy of Norbert Gerling

Very little time passed before the U.S. Army veteran decided to embark upon a life of marital bliss and begin building his own family. As reported in the February 9, 1946 edition of the *Daily Capital News,* Norbert Victor Gerling and Elizabeth Rose Kempker traveled to Jefferson City the previous day to file for their marriage license with the county recorder. On February 23, 1946, during a ceremony held at St. Thomas Catholic Church (in St. Thomas, Missouri), Gerling was united in marriage to his life's love, who had devotedly awaited his return throughout a lengthy overseas deployment.

Following their marriage, the couple purchased a house and farm in Henley, nearby to the farm on which Gerling had been raised. In 1950, they remodeled their home, which, Gerling said, "was built so long ago that no one knows how old it actually is."

His father, Henry A. Gerling, retired from farming and passed away in 1953, only a few short years following his son's release from the U.S. Army. The following year, Gerling's mother, the former Anna Rackers, passed away and was interred next to her husband in the cemetery of the nearby St. Thomas Church.

As the years continued their grind forward, Gerling and his wife went on to raise a family of four children—a son, Bob Gerling; and three daughters, Elaine Lackman, Mary Ann Bax and Donna Junkans. Sadly, on May 2, 1988, Gerling's wife of forty-two years passed away and was laid to rest in the Our Lady of the Snows Cemetery in Mary's Home, Missouri. It was an emotionally devastating event for the once-young soldier who chose to wait until after the war to marry his sweetheart ... just in case he did not make it home. Instead, the devoted husband had to lay his dearly beloved to eternal rest.

Raising a family and working his farm kept Gerling in a state of constant movement for a number of years, but he was often able to find the time to imbibe in a little recreation that was, in a sense, reflective of his service during the late months of his overseas service. For many years of his post-war life, he continued to play baseball for several local teams. Though his participation in the sport waned as he gained a little age, he went on to play again in his late eighties and into his early

Gerling posed for a picture next to the blanket he received as a gift in 2012 while in San Antonio Texas, during one of the final reunions of original members of the 609th Tank Destroyer Battalion – *Courtesy of Jeremy P. Amick*

Jeremy Paul Ämick

nineties in local games that helped raise money for charities such as the American Cancer Society.

When interviewed for this book in 2014 and 2015, the passage of several decades had transpired since Gerling bounced around the insides of a tank destroyer. Regardless, he managed to defy the hands of time by remaining very active, regularly putting in a full day's work on his farm by completing various chores such as cutting his wood for winter and maintaining a bountiful garden. On occasion, he also enjoyed visiting several of the local schools where he embraced the opportunity to share

with the young students his experiences as a tank destroyer traveling across the war-torn European landscape.

The time he spent in combat remained an indelible memory for the veteran, and was the sort of impetus that encouraged members of the former 609th Tank Destroyer Battalion to begin holding reunions in the years following their return home from the war. As Gerling explained, the group held their first reunion in New York in 1952 and continued this tradition until shortly before Gerling's passing.

During a ceremony in the office of Missouri Governor Jeremiah "Jay" Nixon on January 21, 2015, Sergeant Norbert Gerling receives the French Legion of Honor Medal. After the ceremony, Gerling stated that he received the medal "on behalf of the men that I served with in the 609th." – *Courtesy of Shawn C. Johnson*

"I hosted a reunion here in Jefferson City in 2014," Gerling said, "and only me and one other vet showed up: Clarence Blish from Amarillo, Texas. All the others either had passed on or couldn't get around well enough anymore to make the trip. Clarence said that he wouldn't be able to come anymore because he was getting to old for it, so that is kind of the end of it for us." However, Gerling explained, there are many children and grandchildren of the soldiers who served in the 609th who

96

The Lucky Ones

continued to carry on the memory of the organization through other types of events.

The end of reunions, depressing as it may have been for Gerling, also reminded him of a gathering of the 609th from years previous, which he helped plan and coordinate, resulting in a resounding success among his fellow former tank destroyers.

"In 1998, I hosted a big reunion on my son's nearby farm and ninety-two people showed up to it. It was truly a memorable event and it was great to see many of the people I had spent so much time with during the war," he grinned in recollection. "We had people from twenty-five states that came and we served a complete country meal with fried chicken, roast beef, mashed potatoes and green beans. My daughter-in-law baked homemade pies for the whole bunch ... and that was some chore!" he exclaimed.

His golden years, though absent the companionship of his beloved Elizabeth, remained busy with accolades that he was able to enjoy in the presence of both friends and family. On January 21, 2015, nearly seventy years after receiving his award of the Bronze Star medal for his actions in rescuing a stranded tank, Gerling was given another venerated distinction—this time, a quite unanticipated yet venerable recognition from the French government and its citizens for his contributions from decades previous.

"One hour ago, in my office, I presented the Legion of Honor to Norbert Gerling of Henley, Missouri," said Missouri Governor Jeremiah "Jay" Nixon, during his State of the State Address where Gerling was publicly recognized. "It is the

Proudly wearing his ball cap denoting his status as a World War II veteran, Gerling pauses for a photograph with fellow WWII veteran Pete Adkins at the Quilts of Valor Ceremony held at the American Legion in Jefferson City, Missouri in December 2015. Gerling passed away approximately six weeks later. – *Courtesy of Jeremy P. Ämick*

highest distinction bestowed by the French government for service to the people of France." Noting Gerling's service as a gunner aboard a Hellcat during the war, the governor added, "Sergeant Gerling represents millions of members of the Greatest Generation, men and women who demonstrated the grit, courage and unshakeable optimism that made our country what it is today."

With unwavering energy, Gerling remained vigorously involved in a number of activities throughout 2015, not realizing that the abdominal pains he was experiencing foreshadowed an affliction that would soon bring his passing. In November 5, 2015, he joined a small group of World War II veterans that were honored at a USO-style dinner hosted by a local patriotic organization Operation Bugle Boy. The honorees met at a hotel in Jefferson City prior to the evening event and were transported by trolley a few miles west to the Knights of Columbus facility near the community of St. Martins, where the dinner was held. A crowd of more than five hundred local veterans, their spouses and supporters packed the building to listen to the story of Gerling's service and that of the other honorees, such as local Tuskegee Airman James Shipley of Tipton, Missouri.

The following month, on the evening of December 15, Gerling was among a group of six World War II veterans presented with a quilt during a ceremony held at the American Legion Post 5 in Jefferson City. The quilt was an element of the "Quilts of Valor" program that began in 2003 by a mother whose son deployed to Iraq. The quilts were lovingly pieced together by volunteers from the Mid-Missouri Chapter of Quilts of Valor in Columbia, Missouri; the program has chapters engaged in similar activities to honor veterans nationwide. Jan Hobbs, a member of the local chapter, said during the event, "We've awarded 45 quilts this year, which is about the same as we did last year. The quilts are patterned to be specifically detailed showing what the veteran did when they served. We want them to be used and not kept in a corner."[96]

During the patriotic ceremony, Gerling displayed his wry sense of humor while the presenters were reading the history of service of each

---

[96] December 16, 2015 edition of the *Jefferson City News Tribune*.

of the recipients. One veteran who was preparing to receive a quilt had his story shared, in which it was mentioned that he first enlisted in the Marine Corps when he was only fourteen years old by lying about his age; however, his father quickly learned of the unauthorized enlistment and managed to get his son out of the service. After hearing the description of this veteran, Gerling paused, leaned forward, and in the rather loud voice of someone who is hard of hearing stated, "Fourteen years old? I wonder if he packed his diaper bag." Those within earshot of the statement were unable to refrain from chuckling.

Throughout the waning months of 2015, Gerling made frequent mention of discomfort he was experiencing in his abdomen, initially believing it was because of something occurring in his diet. He would adjust his diet and food intake, but when that did not provide any significant level of relief, he scheduled appointments with the local Department of Veterans Affairs medical clinic to determine the source of the discomfort. His pain eventually reached the point that he was sent to the Harry S. Truman Memorial VA Hospital in Columbia, Missouri, in January 2016, where he was diagnosed with colon cancer. Since he was now ninety-six years of age, the doctors realized there could be little done to treat his condition. Contemplating the consequences of the diagnosis, Gerling made the decision to return to his home and enter hospice care.

It was on February 3, 2016, that Gerling made the transition from his temporary earthly abode into eternal rest, passing away in his own bed in the home he had his wife had established shortly after his return from World War II and where they had watched their children grow into adults. Shortly after his death, his body was carried out of the back gate of his home one last time.

"It was very symbolic that they took him out that back gate," said Elaine Lackman, Gerling's oldest daughter. "During his life, he had gone out that gate thousands of times to go to the barn or tend to garden or livestock," she added. "Now, he was making his final journey through that well-worn gate."

His visitation was held on the evening of February 5, 2016 at Our Lady of the Snows Catholic Church in Mary's Home. The following morning, after a funeral mass attended by countless friends and family, the former tank destroyer was laid to rest with full military honors alongside his beloved Elizabeth in the church cemetery.

NORBERT V GERLING
SGT US ARMY
MAY 26 1919   FEB 3 2016

Prior to his death, Gerling was awash with pride when reflecting on his service with the tank destroyers decades earlier. He realized he had been part of a significant moment in armored history that passed away after the closing of the war. Despite the accomplishments, he never sought recognition for himself; instead, he chose to praise those with whom he served, most importantly, those who never came home. Realizing the book chronicling his service in the war would soon be released, he admonished, "I just don't want to sound like I'm bragging—we were all over there just doing our jobs."

During one of the several interviews that took place in the living room of his humble home, he modestly described his time during World War II as "a battle here ... a battle there." Gerling also stated that the actions in which he participated were a "long-range kind of combat not nearly as bad as the boys in the Pacific had it." The former tank destroyer's humility provides true witness and insight to the brave individuals who gave of both their time and youth in defense of the nation, wishing for little more than to finish their jobs in an overseas warzone and to return home to the ones they loved. Gerling's story of service, and those of the other soldiers of the 609th Tank Destroyer Battalion, are inextricably woven into the tapestry of our local communities and continue to serve as lesson in the hardships others have endured in pursuit of a cause they perceived as greater than the individual and for which they did not seek out recognition.

Pictured above are members of the 609th Tank Destroyer Battalion during a reunion held on the farm of Norbert Gerling's son in 1998. Gerling noted that during this event, ninety-two people from twenty-five states were in attendance. Gerling is pictured in the front row, second person to the right of the tank destroyer emblem, wearing a ball cap and with his hands resting on his right knee. –*courtesy of Norbert Gerling*

These men and women of the "Greatest Generation" have become the embodiment of what has made the United States the greatest nation on earth and have gifted us with accounts from their time spent in military uniform—a narrative from the deadly and difficult time known at the Second World War. Too many of these brave individuals surrendered their lives in the pursuit of victory so that their brothers in arms would live to share the stories of the high costs of freedom ... and to ensure that their communities would continue to memorialize those whose return was heralded by flag-draped coffins.

Forged in the cauldron of freedom's fight—Gerling and his fellow crewmembers of the tank destroyers have faced the fires of combat service and learned firsthand of the costs associated with preserving the freedoms the citizens of this country continue to enjoy. If there is one treasure that Gerling cultivated during his more than nine decades of life experiences, it is the bounty of hard-earned wisdom and insight gained alongside a generation of Americans who have all but disappeared.

"You just never worried ...even when you were in combat," he affirmed. "Your primary concern was winning the war and then coming home. We were trained to face anything, and there were times when you saw your buddies pretty well butchered up, but you didn't worry about it [at that time] because you had a mission to accomplish."

With the pause of a battle-hardened soldier that has witnessed the worst of humanity in a combat zone thousands of miles of home, far removed from family, Gerling affirmed, "We were the entire history of the battalion; it formed after basic training and it was disbanded after we got back home—but we were the tank destroyers."

Softly, he concluded, "But as I always said, I was one of the lucky ones ... I got to come home when so many others did not."

The End

The Lucky Ones

Norbert V. Gerling

May 25, 1919 – February 3, 2016

Appendix A

According to the battalion history of the 609th Tank Destroyer Battalion compiled by the late Albert F. Ahrenholz, the following dates and locations represent the various command posts used by the battalion.[97]

***

609th Tank Destroyer Battalion
Command Post (CP) Locations

Camp Shanks, New York (POE)	3 Aug '44
Liverpool, England	24 Aug '44
Llanover Park, England	24 Aug '44
Dorchester, England	16 Sep '44
Portland, England	19 Sep '44
Utah Beach, France	20 Sep '44

---

[97] Albert F. Ahrenholz was a member of the 609th Tank Destroyer Battalion from August 24, 1942 through July 2, 1945. From August 1942 through July 1943, Ahrenholz served as a platoon leader and executive officer for Company A; from July 1943 through August 1943, he served as the commander of Headquarters Company; from August 1943 through June 1945, he served as the commander of Company B; and, from June 1945 through July 1945, he served as a staff officer in the Headquarters and Headquarters Company. Following World War II, he continued his military service, which included brigade commander in the Second Infantry Division in Korea and deputy commander of Ft. Gordon, Georgia. On August 1, 1974, he retired from active duty at the rank of colonel after having served thirty-four years in uniform. His awards include the Legion of Merit with two oak leaf clusters; the Bronze Star medal; Joint Services Commendation medal, the Purple Heart; and the European Theater of Operations Ribbon with four campaign stars. The combat veteran passed away on February 26, 2004 and is buried in Beaufort National Cemetery in South Carolina.

Jeremy Paul Ämick

St. Mere Eglise, France .... 21 Sep '44
Longey, France .... 22 Sep '44
Sens, France .... 23 Sep '44
St. Menehold, France .... 26 Sep '44
Moutiers, France (entered action) .... 27 Sep '44
Vionville, France .... 3 Nov '44
Puxieux, France .... 3 Nov '44
Ottange, France .... 9 Nov '44
Maginot Line, France .... 15 Nov '44
Malling, France .... 17 Nov '44
Kaltviller, France .... 18 Nov '44
Rustroff, France .... 28 Nov '44
Garnich, Luxembourg .... 18 Dec '44
Merl, Luxembourg .... 18 Dec '44
Beringen, Luxembourg .... 21 Dec '44
Rodenbourg, Luxembourg .... 10 Jan '45
Colligny, France .... 11 Jan '45
Dieuze, France .... 17 Jan '45
Teting, France .... 22 Jan '45
Bechy, France .... 29 Jan '45
Metz, France .... 10 Feb '45
Sierk, France .... 20 Feb '45
Besch, France .... 20 Feb '45
Wincherringen, Germany .... 21 Feb '45
Nittel, Germany .... 22 Feb '45
Beurig, Germany .... 27 Feb '45
Trier, Germany .... 3 Mar '45
Waldrach, Germany .... 18 Mar '45
Thalfang, Germany .... 19 Mar '45
Wirschweiler, Germany .... 20 Mar '45
Saarlautern, Germany .... 23 Mar '45
Edenkoben, Germany .... 24 Mar '45
Queichheim, Germany .... 25 Mar '45
Sandofen, Germany .... 29 Mar '45
Rohrbach, Germany .... 1 Apr '45

The Lucky Ones

Bad Rappenau, Germany .... 4 Apr '45
Hungheim, Germany .... 6 Apr '45
Assamstadt, Germany .... 7 Apr '45
Diebach, Germany .... 12 Apr '45
Ohringen, Germany .... 14 Apr '45
Bead Castell, Germany .... 18 Apr '45
Fornsbach, Germany .... 19 Apr '45
Aldorf, Germany .... 20 Apr '45
Faurndau, Germany .... 21 Apr '45
Laichingen, Germany .... 23 Apr '45
Ehingen, Germany .... 24 Apr '45
Laupheim, Germany .... 24 Apr '45
Unter Balzheim, Germany .... 25 Apr '45
Mindelheim, Germany .... 27 Apr '45
Schongau, Germany .... 28 Apr '45
Garmisch-Partenkirchen, Germany .... 30 Apr '45
Kochel, Germany .... 15 May '45

Appendix B

Below is the copy of the general order which awarded a unit citation to the 101st Airborne Division and elements of the 609th Tank Destroyer Battalion for their participation in the Battle of the Bulge.

***

HEADQUARTERS
THIRD UNITED STATES ARMY
APO 403

General Orders .... 7 February 1945
Number 31

UNIT CITATION

Under the provisions of Section IV, Circular 633, War Department, 22 December 1943 and in accordance with the authority contained in War Department cable W-24 608, 21 January 1945, the following units are cited:

101st Airborne Division (less 2nd Battalion, 401st Glider Infantry Regiment) with the following attached units:

****

Company C: 609th Tank Destroyer Battalion (less 1st Platoon; with 2nd Platoon Reconnaissance Company attached.

These units distinguished themselves in combat against powerful and aggressive enemy forces composed of elements of eight German Divisions during the period of 18 December to 27 December 1944, by extraordinary heroism and gallantry in defense of the key communications center of Bastogne, Belgium. Essential to a large-scale exploitation of his breakthrough into Belgium and northern Luxembourg, the enemy attempted to seize Bastogne by attacking constantly and savagely with the best of his armor and infantry. Without benefit of prepared defenses, facing almost overwhelming odds and with very limited and fast-dwindling supplies, these units maintained a high combat morale and impenetrable defense, despite extremely heavy bombing, intense artillery fire and constant attacks from infantry and armor on all sides of their completely cut-off and encircled position. This masterful and grimly determined defense denied the enemy even momentary success in an operation for which he paid dearly in men, material and eventually morale. The outstanding courage, resourcefulness and undaunted determination of this gallant force are in keeping with the highest tradition of the Service.

By Command of Lieutenant General Patton:

HOBART R. GAY
Brigadier General, U.S. Army
Chief of Staff

Official:

R.E. Cummings,
Colonel, Adjutant Generals Department
Adjutant General

Appendix C

Below is a copy of the narrative from the military order awarding Norbert Gerling with a Bronze Star medal.

***

Sergeant Norbert VJ Gerling 37084735, Company C, 609th Tank Destroyer Battalion, United States Army, for heroic achievement in connection with military operations against an enemy of the United States at Trier, Germany on 7 March 1945. When a friendly tank was disabled by intense anti-tank fire, Sergeant Gerling, gunner, voluntarily exposing himself, brought continuous fire upon the enemy position, enabling the tank crew to reach a place of safety. His exemplary conduct reflects great credit upon himself and the military forces of the United States. Entered the military service from St. Thomas, Missouri.

Appendix D

Below is a copy of the narrative report highlighting operations that pertain to the event Gerling recalled occurring in the area of Noville, Belgium during the Battle of the Bulge.

***

SUBJECT: HIGHLIGHTS OF OPERATIONS 609th TD BATTALION
Period: 15th November – 31st December 1944

TO: Commanding Officer
1st Tank Destroyer Brigade (Att'n Major Orman S-3)

(The first several paragraphs of this report pertaining to 609th's Reconnaissance Company and Companies A & B have been removed for abridgement purposes.)

Company "C", was contacted for the first time on the 28th December since their departure to BASTOGNE pocket on the 18th December. Fifteen enemy Mk Vs and one Mk VI as well as three AT SP Guns were known to have been destroyed. Fourteen of these tanks were destroyed during the period 20th – 21st December by 3rd Platoon under command of 1st Lt. David K. Hagens in the vicinity of NOVILLE (P588646) Belgium. The attacking enemy tanks were engaged as they emerged from the heavy fog at ranges of 200-300 yards. One destroyer knocked out five Mk Vs with six rounds. Lt. Hagens employed two destroyers in static positions with excellent field of fire and took advantage of buildings in NOVILLE for cover. The other two destroyers of his platoon roved about the village and were prepared to move into numerous positions upon call from either Lt. Hagens or Platoon Sgt. Mays.

The second platoon, commanded by Lt. Edward Gladden was successfully employed in direct fire at enemy infantry to repel counterattacks. It was while breaking u one of the enemy's persistent counterattacks, that Gladden's platoon destroyed a Mk V Tank with an M-10 Destroyer which was manned by a makeshift crew composed of personnel from Company Headquarters. The M-10 had been recovered under fire, manned and employed successfully.

The Recon Platoon, commanded by 1st Lt. M.K. Grant operated directly with elements of the 101st A/B Division and was outposting the BASTOGNE-ARLON Highway.

Casualties sustained to date in the BASTOGNE pocket were 13 men and 8 vehicles, (2 M-18s, 2 M-20s, 3 ¼ Tons and 1 2-1/2 Ton Truck). These losses were principally the result of the intensive nightly enemy bombings to which the company was subjected. Two of the men killed were slightly wounded in action however aerial bombing Christmas night caught them in the hospital resulting in their deaths.

The company accounted for 48 Prisoners of War and killed an estimated 150 enemy troops.

                For the Commanding Officer

                            WILLIAM H. HATINA,
                            Major, FA (TD)
                            S-3

Appendix E

Below is a copy of the letter Gerling received from the French Consulate in Chicago advising him of the award of the French Legion of Honor.

Jeremy Paul Ämick

**CONSULAT GENERAL DE FRANCE
A
CHICAGO**

Chicago, December 17, 2014

Dear Mr. Gerling,

It is a great honor and privilege to present you with the Knight of the Legion of Honor medal. Through this award, the French government pays tribute to the soldiers who did so much for France and Western Europe. 70 years ago, you gave your youth to France and the French people. Many of your fellow soldiers did not return but they remain in our hearts.

Thanks to your courage, and to our American friends and allies, France and Europe have been living in peace for the past seven decades. You saved us. We will never forget. For us, the French people, you are heroes. Gratitude and remembrance are forever in our souls.

To show our eternal gratitude, the government of the French Republic has decided to award you the Legion of Honor. Created by Napoleon, it is the highest honor that France can bestow upon those who have achieved remarkable deeds for France.

Thank you for what you did and congratulations.

Sincerely yours,

Vincent FLOREANI
Consul Général de France à Chicago

WORKS CITED

NEWSPAPERS

Acadiana Advocate (Baton Rouge, Louisiana)
Daily Capital News (Jefferson City, Missouri)
Daily Republican (Monongahela, Pennsylvania)
Fayetteville Observer (Fayetteville, North Carolina)
Florence Morning News (Florence, South Carolina)
Jefferson City News Tribune (Jefferson City, Missouri)
Jefferson City Post-Tribune (Jefferson City, Missouri)
Pittsburgh Post-Gazette (Pittsburgh, Pennsylvania)
Portland Press Herald (Portland, Maine)
New York Times (New York, New York)
San Francisco Examiner (San Francisco, California)
Waukesha Daily Freeman (Waukesha, Wisconsin)

BOOKS AND ARTICLES

Ambrose, Stephen. *The Supreme Commander: The War Years of Dwight D. Eisenhower*. (New York: Anchor Books, 1969).

Baker, Sergeant George. *The Sad Sack: His Biography in 115 Cartoons from the Pages of Yank Magazine*. (New York: Simon and Schuster, 1944).

Barron, Leo & Don Cygan. *No Silent Night: The Christmas Battle for Bastogne*. (New York: Penguin Group, 2012).

Baxter, John. *When Disney Went to War*. (Air & Space Magazine, February 5, 2015).

Briley, Ron (Editor). *The Politics of Baseball: Essays on the Pastime and Power at Home and Abroad.* (Jefferson, NC: McFarland & Company, Inc., 2010).

Frederick L. Briue. "FORT HOOD," *Handbook of Texas Online* (http://www.tshaonline.org/handbook/online/articles/qbf25), accessed May 27, 2015. Uploaded on June 12, 2010. Published by the Texas State Historical Association.

Chapman Dean M. *Growl of the Tiger: Tenth Armored Division's Epic Stories of Combat in World War II in Europe.* (Paducah, KY: Turner Publishing Company, 1993).

Colley, David P. *The Road to Victory: The Untold Story of World War II's Red Ball Express.* (New York: Warner Books, Inc., 2000).

Collins, Michael and Martin King. *The Tigers of Bastogne: Voices of the 10th Armored Division in the Battle of the Bulge.* (Havertown, PA: Casemate Publishers, 2013).

Corsi, Jerome. *No Greater Valor: The Siege of Bastogne, and the Miracle that Sealed Allied Vistory.* (Nashville, Tenn: Thomas Nelson, 2014).

Cross, Walt. *Tank Busters—The History of the 607th Tank Destroyer Battalion.* (Stillwater, Okla: Dire Wolf Books, 2010).

Dungan, T.D. *V-2: A Combat History of the First Ballistic Missile.* (Yardley, Pennsylvania: Westholme Publishing, 2005).

Green, Michael. *American Tanks and AFVs of World War II.* (Oxford, UK: Osprey Publishing, 2014).

Green, Michael and Gladys. *Panther: Germany's Quest for Combat Dominance.* (Oxford, UK: Osprey Publishing, 2012).

Heaton, Colin & Anne-Marie Lewis. *The Me 262 Stormbird: From the Pilots Who Flew, Fought, and Survived It.* (Minneapolis, MN: Zenith Press, 2012).

Diana J. Kleiner, "BRUCE, ANDREW DAVIS," *Handbook of Texas Online* (http://www.tshaonline.org/handbook/online/articles/fbrbq), accessed May 27, 2015. Uploaded on June 12, 2010. Published by the Texas State Historical Association

Lucas, Richard. *Axis Sally: The American Voice of Nazi Germany*. (Havertown, PA: Casemate, 2013).

Lowe, Christopher. *Farming in the Great Depression*. Pickler Memorial Library - Chariton Collector (Spring 1986). Accessed June 12, 2015. http://library.truman.edu/scpublications/chariton%20collector/Spring%201986/Farming%20in%20the%20Great%20Depression.pdf/

MacDonald, Charles B. *The Last Offensive*. (Florence, AL: Whitman Publishing, 2012).

Marshall, S.L.A. *Bastogne: The Story of the First Eight Days*. (Washington, D.C: Infantry Journal Press, 1946).

McCallum, Jack. *Military Medicine: From Ancient Times to the 21st Century*. (Santa Barbara, CA: ABC-CLIO, Inc., 2008).

Miller, Francis Trevelyan. *History of World War II*. (Philadelphia: The John C. Winston Company, 1945).

U.S. War Department. *Tank Destroyer Field Manual: Organization and Tactics of Tank Destroyer Units*. (Washington, D.C.: United States Government Printing Office, 1942).

Wright, Stephen L. *The Last Drop: Operation Varsity, March 24-25, 1945*. (Mechanicsburg, PA: Stackpole Books, 2008).

Zalgoa, Steven J. *Eisenhower*. (Oxford, UK: Osprey Publishing, 2011).

Zalgoa, Steven J. *US Amphibious Tanks of World War II*. (Oxford, UK: Osprey Publishing, 2012).

ONLINE RESOURCES

1920 US Census, www.archives.com.

1930 US Census, www.archives.com.

Field, F.P. *The Capture of Wernher Von Braun.* Accessed September 1, 2015. http://www.12tharmoredmuseum.com/capture.asp.

After Action Reports. *284th Field Artillery Battalion During World War II.* Accessed June 4, 2015. http://284thfabn.com/helpmate.pdf.

Archives.org. *FM 18-5: Organization and Tactics of Tank Destroyer Units.* Accessed June 1,

2015. https://archive.org/stream/Fm18-5#page/n0/mode/2up.

Baseball Almanac. *1944 World Series.* Accessed July 9, 2015. http://www.baseball-almanac.com/ws/yr1944ws.shtml.

Baseball-Reference.com. *Stan Musial.* Accessed September 12, 2015. http://www.baseball-reference.com/players/m/musiast01.shtml.

Baseball-Reference.com. *St. Louis Browns.* Accessed October 14, 2015. http://www.baseball-reference.com/bullpen/St. Louis Browns.

Encyclopedia of World Biography. *Wernher Von Braun Biography.* Accessed September 1, 2015. http://www.notablebiographies.com/Tu-We/Von-Braun-Wernher.html.

France in the United States: Embassy of France in Washington, D.C. *France Honors American World War Veterans.* Accessed May 31, 2015. http://ambafrance-us.org/spip.php?article3150.

Fort Bragg. *Fort Bragg History.* Accessed May 30, 2015. http://www.bragg.army.mil/Pages/History.aspx.

Foster, Renita. "'Yank' Magazine Energized Soldiers, Reminded Them of the Reasons for Fighting." *Fort Monmouth Public Affairs* (August 20, 2009*).* Accessed July 8, 2015. http://www.army.mil/article/26343/_039_Yank_039_magazine_energized_Soldiers_reminding_them_of_the_reasons_for_fighting/.

Germany History Documents. *The Cross of Honor for the German Mother*. Retrieved September 1, 2015. http://germanhistorydocs. ghi-dc.org/sub_image.cfm?image_id=2044.

Harry S. Truman Library and Museum. 70th Anniversary of the End of World War II. Accessed May 20, 2015. https://www.trumanlibrary.org/wwii/V-EDayCommemoration.pdf.

History.com. *8 Things You Should Know About WWII's Eastern Front*. Accessed July 9, 2015. http://www.history.com/news/history-lists/8-things-you-should-know-about-wwiis-eastern-front.

Hudson River Valley National Heritage Area. *Camp Shanks World War II Museum*. Accessed June 3, 2015. http://www.hudsonrivervalley.com/Details.aspx?sid=c5a8c9f0-fa2d-4e53-8fad-dfe0124188c4.

King, Martin. *African Nurse Save GIs at Battle of the Bulge*. U.S. Army News Archives (February 18, 2011). http://www.army.mil/article/52148/.

Jefferson Barracks Community Council. *History of Jefferson Barracks*. Accessed May 30, 2015. http://jbccstl.org.

MilitaryBases.Com. *Camp Shelby Army Base in Hattiesburg, MS*. Accessed May 28, 2015.

http://militarybases.com/camp-shelby-army-base-in-hattiesburg-ms/.

MilitaryFactory.com. *M3 37mm AT 37mm Anti-Tank Gun (1940)*. Accessed May 26, 2015. http://www.militaryfactory.com/armor/detail.asp?armor_id=329.

MilitaryFactory.com. *M3 Gun Motor Carriage (75mm) Half-track Tank Destroyer* (1941). Accessed May 26, 2015. http://www.militaryfactory.com/armor/detail.asp?armor_id=738.

Missouri Death Certificates. Missouri Digital Heritage.

http://www.sos.mo.gov/archives/resources/deathcertificates/#searchdeat

Missouri Digital Heritage. *O'Reilly General Hospital of Springfield, Missouri*. Accessed July 22, 2015. http://cdm16795.contentdm.oclc.org/cdm/landingpage/collection/oreillyhosp.

Missouri Soldiers' Database: War of 1812-WWI. Missouri Digital Heritage.

www.sos.mo.gov/mdh/CivilWar/Resources.asp

My Germany City. *Crailsheim—City of Resilience, Risen from the Ashes*. Accessed August 12, 2015. http://www.mygermancity.com/crailsheim.

National World War II Museum. *The Draft and WWII*. Accessed June 16, 2015. http://www.nationalww2museum.org/learn/education/for-students/ww2-history/take-a-closer-look/draft-registration-documents.html.

NavSource Online. *USS Hermitage (AP-54)*. Accessed June 3, 2015. http://www.navsource.org/archives/09/22/22054.htm.

TankDestroyer.net. *Biography of Justin Deryl Double*. Accessed July 20, 2015. http://www.tankdestroyer.net/honorees/d/526-double-justin-d-609th.

Terrify and Destroy: The Story of the 10th Armored Division. (Published by the *Star & Stripes* magazine in Paris 1944-1945). Accessed on July 31, 2015. http://www.lonesentry.com/gi_stories_booklets/10tharmored/

The Acadian Museum. *Living Legends: Brigadier General Robert LeBlanc*. Accessed May 28, 2015. http://www.acadianmuseum.com/legends.php?viewID=100.

The Armored School at Ft. Knox, Kentucky. *10th Armored Division in the Crailsheim Operation. A research report prepared by committee 8 officers at the advance course at the Armored* School, 1949-195). Accessed August 15, 2015. http://cgsc.contentdm.oclc.org/cdm/ref/collection/p4013coll8/id/3199.

The Battle of Normandy. *Landing Ship Tank (LST) Mk2*. Accessed June 15, 2015. http://www.dday-overlord.com/eng/landing_ship_tank.htm.

The Outpost Harry Survivors Association. *Distinguished Unit Citations*. Accessed October 14, 2015. http://www.ophsa.org/DUC/.

U.S. Marine Corps. *Bulk Fuel Operations*. (MCWP 4-11.6, 29 August 1996). Accessed June 30, 2015. http://www.trngcmd.marines.mil/Portals/207/Docs/TBS/MCWP%204-11.6%20Bulk%20Liquid%20Operations.pdf.

The 85th in German—Official Unit History. *The Rhineland Operation*. Accessed July 25, 2015. http://www.85th-engineer.com/319115463.

Verndale, Minnesota. *Gen. Lesley J. McNair*. Accessed June 1, 2015. http://www.verndalemn.com/McNair.html.

Warfare History Network. *WWII Weapons: The German 88mm Gun*. Accessed January 9, 2018. https://warfarehistorynetwork.com/daily/wwii/wwii-weapons-the-german-88mm-gun/.

INDEX

Adkins, Pete, 97
Baker, Sgt. George, 43-45
Bax, Mary Ann, 95
Bayless, William "Lacey", 20
Beaster, Richard, 59-60
Blish, Clarence, 96
Bragg, Braxton, 9
Bruce, Gen. Andrew, 12-14
Chapman, Dean, 61
Chorak, Capt. Stephen, 29, 32
DiSanza, Victor, 89-90
Disney, Walt, 16-17, 44
Double, Justin, 53-55
Eisenhower, Gen. Dwight, 38, 47, 50
Gaffney, Bud, 73
Gerling, Anna, 3
Gerling, Bob, 95
Gerling, Elizabeth, 94
Gerling, Henry, 4, 95
Gerling, Hubert, 19-20
Gerling, Martha, 3
Gerling, Matilda, 3
Gerling, Micheal, 4
Gerling, Rose, 3
Gillars, Mildred, 42
Graybeal, Raymond, 33
Herigon, Raymond, 45
Hitler, Adolf, 50-52, 83, 86-87

Hobbs, Jan, 98
Huhman, Agnes, 20
Hutchinson, Clem, 70
Iler, Alan, 33, 56-58
Jones, Myrna, 3
Junkans, Donna, 95
Keith, Emylou, 72-74
Kempker, Elizabeth, 6-7, 25, 63, 92
Kuktis, Charlie, 33, 84
Lackman, Elaine, 95, 99
LeBlanc, Brig. Gen. Robert, 2-3
Maher, Robert, 20
McNair, Gen. Lesley J., 14
Mosetti, Sgt. Joseph, 78
Musial, Stan, 89-90
Nilges, Herman, 6
Nilges, Marcellus, 3
Nilges, Sarah, 6
Nixon, Gov. Jeremiah "Jay", xi, 93, 96-97
Patton, General George S., 2, 35-36, 38, 47, 50, 58, 110
Pershing, Gen. John J., 35
Rackers, Anna, 95
Ricker, Colby, 53-55
Roat Jr., John, 33
Roosevelt, Pres. Franklin D., 7-8
Sanders, John Hubert, 69

Jeremy Paul Ämick

Seech, Sgt. Nicholas, 82
Sherman, Phillip, 20
Shipley, James, 98
Smith, Mildred Elizabeth (Axis Sally) 42

Stihl, Maxine, 56
Stihl, Michael, 56
Suber, Floyd, 70-74
Truman, Pres. Harry S., 2, 83, 86, 99
Von Braun, Wernher, 39, 87-88

CPSIA information can be obtained
at www.ICGtesting.com
Printed in the USA
FFHW011925200219
50621299-55996FF